ETHICS IN ELECTROCONVULSIVE THERAPY

JAN-OTTO OTTOSSON, M.D., Ph.D.
MAX FINK, M.D.

Brunner-Routledge
New York • Hove

Published in 2004 by
Brunner-Routledge
29 West 35th Street
New York, NY 10001
www.brunner-routledge.com

Published in Great Britain by
Brunner-Routledge
27 Church Road
Hove, East Sussex
BN3 2FA
www.brunner-routledge.co.uk

Printed in the United States of America on acid-free paper.
Typesetting: BookType

10 9 8 7 6 5 4 3 2 1

Library of Congress Cataloging-in-Publication Data

Ottosson, Jan-Otto.
    Ethics in Electroconvulsive therapy / Jan-Otto Ottosson,
Max Fink.
        p.   cm.
Includes bibliographical references and index.
    ISBN 0-415-94659-X (hardback)
    1. Electroconvulsive therapy—Moral and ethical aspects.
    [DNLM: 1. Electroconvulsive therapy—ethics. WM 410 O91e 2004]
I. Fink, Max, 1923– II. Title.
RC485.O88 2004
616.89'122—dc22

                                            2003025759

Contents

List of Patient Vignettes

Preface

Although we have worked in the different health care systems of Sweden and the United States, we have had similar tasks as clinicians, researchers, and as educators of medical students and specialists in psychiatry. As far as possible we have offered evidence-based care and treatment for patients with widely different mental disorders. To one effective treatment, that of electroconvulsive therapy (ECT) we have often met irrational attitudes. Not only from patients and their relatives, but also from medical specialists, even fellow psychiatrists. In some venues, the attitudes against the use of ECT have been so strong as to stimulate a political response with ensuing legal restrictions. At times, the treatment has been stamped as unethical. Despite evidence of its efficacy and safety, it has been widely underutilized, to the disadvantage of patients, their families, and to health care budgets.

ECT has been a common interest for us and we developed a collaboration and friendship for more than 40 years. We share a common experience that the known facts about ECT have been only partially successful in limiting irrationality, discomfort, and stigmatization.

Modern biomedical ethics developed in reaction to violations to human rights that were so prominent throughout the 20th century. The interest in ethics has yielded codes for clinical research and health care to guide health care professionals. In addition to codes of conduct, medical ethicists have developed methods for analyzing which actions are preferable in various health care situations.

With a desire to clarify the controversies that swirl about ECT, we present an ethical analysis of ECT for health care professionals, students, and the public. The high incidence of mental disorders makes it likely that almost all readers will have been confronted with the offer of ECT or other controversial treatment for themselves or a member of their family. The ethical analysis of ECT is broadly applicable to all medical interventions.

With gratitude, we acknowledge advice from Alfred M. Freedman, M.D., Norton Spritz, M.D., J.D., and George Zimmar, Ph.D., of New York, John Little, M.D. of Australia, and Barry Martin, M.D. of Canada who read early drafts of this work.

Jan-Otto Ottosson
Max Fink

Introduction

Electroconvulsive therapy (ECT, convulsive therapy, electroshock) was introduced in the 1930s at a time when no effective treatment for the severe mentally ill was known. It was received enthusiastically, applied widely, and recognized as particularly effective in relieving depression, mania, psychosis, and suicide risk of schizophrenia and manic depressive illness. Within two decades, however, it became the center of a controversy that stigmatized and severely restricted its use (Fink, 1979, 1991, 1997; Lebensohn, 1984; Shorter, 1997; Kneeland & Warren, 2002). It was replaced by new psychoactive drugs but as drug treatments increasingly failed to relieve many psychiatric illnesses, ECT use increased, encouraged by its rapid efficacy and reduced side effects occasioned by improved techniques and methods (Royal College of Psychiatrists [RCP], 1989; American Psychiatric Association [APA], 1978, 1990, 2001; Abrams, 2002; Scottish ECT Audit Network [SEAN], 2002).

The experience of more than 70 years acknowledges the efficacy of ECT for major depressive disorder, particularly the psychotic form; malignant catatonia in various forms; psychoses labeled acute schizophrenia; manic disorders; and stupors associated with inanition. For some conditions, ECT is the most effective treatment with a well documented record of saving lives (Abrams, 2002; APA, 2001; Fink, 1999; Fink & Taylor, 2003; Ottosson, 2004). This broad efficacy will come as a surprise to many readers who may consider ECT as outmoded and discarded.

The central event in ECT is the repeated induction of grand mal seizures that are elicited two to three times a week in a course of 4 to 12, sometimes up to 20, treatments. Patients are fully anesthetized and relaxed during each induction. The relief of suicide risk and inanition is rapid, often seen within two weeks. Improvements in mood and psychotic thinking quickly follow. These benefits are achieved in shorter time and with greater remission rates than with alternative treatments, (APA, 2001; Abrams, 2002; UK ECT Review Group, 2003).

The controversies that affect ECT are not about its efficacy but about undue risks and allegations of abuse. Critics complain that the effects on memory are so severe, so persistent, and so interfering with a normal life that interdiction of the treatment is the only safe course of action (Friedberg, 1976; Frank, 1978; Breggin, 1979, 1991; Kneeland & Warren, 2002). The critics do not consider that modern methods have considerably relieved the effects on memory nor that the use is largely confined to patients who have failed other interventions. Indeed, ECT is widely applied as the "treatment of last resort." The critics also fail to consider that ECT has some well-defined primary indications (APA, 2001; Abrams, 2002; SEAN, 2002). Legislatures and courts have so burdened access to ECT as to effectively deny it for patients for whom it would have been the appropriate treatment. In some nations, public and professional antipathy has so cowed practitioners that they do not consider ECT an option in the care of their patients and use it rarely.

Critics describe patients as unwilling subjects who are forced to the treatments against their will. Such complaints are a holdover from a much earlier era when the approach to patients was more authoritarian and with little attention to patient autonomy (Grob, 1994; Berrios & Porter, 1995; Shorter, 1997; Porter, 2002). Attitudes to patient autonomy have changed fundamentally, with patients increasingly empowered to make decisions about all aspects of their health care. These attitudes affect ECT as well. In modern practice the consent process recognizes the importance of patient autonomy. ECT is given primarily to competent patients who consent voluntarily. The consent is documented in a formal signed and witnessed document. Occasionally, ECT is given to incompetent patients without their consent when the urgency to protect life is great and the treatment is seen as most appropriate. At such times, the treatment is administered under state regulations written to provide effective care for all patients (APA, 1978, 1991, 2002; Fink, 1979; Abrams, 1988; RCP, 1995).

Ethical analyses have contributed to the development of guidelines for the care of the terminally ill and the use of involuntary commitment. We dare to hope that an ethical approach may throw light on the difficulties in ensuring the use of ECT and even reduce the controversies that swirl about it.

CHAPTER 1

The Stigmatization
of Electroconvulsive Therapy

The stigmatization of ECT has many roots—in fears of electricity and of epileptic seizures, in competing ideologies within psychiatric practice, in the association with old-fashioned health care, and well-meant but misdirected desires of medical personnel to abide by public opinion. Many complain that ECT is overused and misused. When a physician discusses ECT with a patient and the family, the recommendation elicits many concerns and is often rejected. To avoid conflict, physicians delay the recommendation for ECT until all other means, even many with lesser efficacy and unproven safety, have been tried and failed and the illness has become severe and persistent.

Claims of misuse, concerns about the properties of the treatment, ideological conflicts within psychiatry, and economic factors dominate its stigmatization.

Claims of Misuse

Convulsive therapy, in the form of chemically induced seizures, was first tested in the 1930s in patients with dementia praecox, a disorder that is now widely labeled as schizophrenia. While the benefits were immediately obvious in patients with acute forms of the illness, and especially with the catatonic variety, the trials in patients with chronic schizophrenia failed. In other disorders, such as alcoholism, drug abuse, hysteria (conversion reaction), and anxiety states, ECT did not benefit the patients. In patients with obsessive compulsive disorders, the benefits were transient. These illnesses did not become indications for its use (Sargant & Slater, 1962; Kalinowsky & Hippius, 1969; APA, 1978; Fink, 1979). By contrast, in patients with involutional melancholia, an often fatal disorder, the results were gratifying and ECT immediately became the accepted treatment (Ziskind et al., 1945; Bond,

1954a; Bond & Morris, 1954b). The benefits in patients with malignant catatonia, psychotic depression, and manic delirium were later defined and were so great as to encourage the frequent and primary use of ECT for these conditions (Fink, 1999; APA, 2001; Abrams, 2002; Fink & Taylor, 2003).

Experimentation in diverse conditions to define the indications for any new treatment is by no means unique for ECT. It is a feature of all new medical discoveries. After the hormone insulin was identified as effective in diabetes, it was tried in many other conditions including the relief of withdrawal of opiate dependence and in schizophrenia. As schizophrenia did not respond to sub-coma doses, higher doses, sufficient to induce states of coma were tested and found to be sometimes effective. Insulin coma therapy was an accepted treatment for psychosis for two decades until it was replaced by antipsychotic drugs (Fink, 2003). Another example is seen in trials of penicillin for infections associated with war wounds. Trials in patients with syphilis led to the discovery that the spirochaete was uniquely sensitive to penicillin and to the remarkable eradication of both the acute and chronic forms of the illness. These trials were considered a remarkable success despite the occurrence of fatal complications (Quétel, 1990).

Overuse of Treatment

Before penicillin, the treatments of syphilis included poisonous arsenicals and the periodic fevers of malaria. The success of malaria therapy, with its fevers occurring in 48 to 96 hour intervals, was hailed as a major advance in medical care, for which the 1927 Nobel Prize in Medicine was awarded. The frequency of malarial fevers and their apparent success became the model for the first attempts at convulsive therapy (Meduna, 1937). As more experience was gained, other treatment frequencies for ECT were examined. If two and three seizures a week were effective, perhaps daily treatments would be more so? Regressive ECT, in which patients were treated daily or twice daily, was tested. The benefits, however, did not occur earlier than with conventional treatment frequencies. The appearance of severe confusional syndromes, occasionally persistent, discouraged this form of ECT and it was abandoned (Fink, 1979; Kalinowsky et al., 1982; APA, 1978, 1990).

In multiple monitored ECT, from four to eight seizures were induced in one morning under one anesthesia, in the hope that the benefits would be superior to the two to three week schedules then in use (Blachly & Gowing, 1976). Only a few patients benefited from this intensive procedure but more patients developed a delirium that was severe and persistent (Abrams & Fink, 1972). This method of ECT was also abandoned (APA, 1978, 1990).

Experiments using varying dosages are a feature of all medical treatments. In the assessment of neuroleptic drugs, high doses, even mega-doses, have been tested and while some benefits were noted, they are only occasionally used today (DiMascio & Shader, 1972; Riker et al., 1994; Hurford, 1999). Radiation and toxic chemical treatments for malignant tumors are another example of the achievement of a reasonable balance between benefits and side effects (Vaeth, 1979; van Houtte et al., 1999). Despite occasional severe side effects, high dose neuroleptic dosing for the severe psychiatrically ill, and radiation and toxic chemical treatments of cancer are accepted by physicians and their patients. Neither course of treatment is stigmatized.

Association with Forced Incarceration

By the first half of the 20th century, most treatments of the psychiatrically ill were carried out in large psychiatric hospitals. According to accepted medical practice, physicians were authorized to compel hospital care for patients considered dangerous to themselves or to others. Such legal commitment was usually in state supported institutions, many of which were overcrowded, inadequately staffed, underfunded, and poorly managed (Deutsch, 1937; Hunter & Macalpine, 1982; Grob, 1994; Shorter, 1997; Ottosson, 2003). The power to commit patients to hospitals and to forcefully treat them was a derived power of the state to protect its citizens. The rules were lax and claims of abuse common. The introduction of such complex treatments as fever therapy, prolonged sleep, insulin coma, convulsive therapy, and lobotomy put overwhelming burdens on the nurses, aides, and physicians in the state facilities. Patients frequently attacked each other and the professional staff, damaged furnishings, smeared walls and floors, and set fires. One of the first evidences of the usefulness of chlorpromazine and other antipsychotic drugs was in the reduction in attacks on personnel and other patients, windows broken, and fires set (Kalinowsky & Hippius, 1969; Sargant & Slater, 1964).

Overuse of isolation rooms, physical restraints, and hot and cold baths to manage unruly patients were frequently reported in the public press. Such management techniques and the intrusive treatments could be administered at the order of the medical staff and without individual consent (Deutsch, 1937, 1946; Grob, 1994; Braslow, 1997). Indeed, the justification for admission to a psychiatric hospital was that the necessary treatments would be applied. Despite widespread complaints of abuse, forced hospitalization and forced treatments were tolerated when physicians were viewed as healers committed to serving the better interests of their patients and justified by the principles of the Hippocratic Oath as it was then interpreted.

In the latter half of the 20th century, however, after two world wars and the controversial conflict for Americans in Vietnam, the public openly questioned the authority of the state to force its will on its citizens. One nidus for this conflict was the forced conscription of men for military service in an undeclared and illegal war. The challenge to authority broadened to include questions whether the state had power to incarcerate individuals for behavior that it deemed dangerous. Reports of the use of commitment procedures to imprison dissidents and force psychiatric medications in the Soviet Union and China raised questions whether these same powers were being abused in the United States. Writers questioned the concepts of psychiatric illness and argued that in forcibly hospitalizing patients, physicians were acting as agents of the state in a fashion that was no different than the behavior of physicians in totalitarian societies (Szasz, 1961, 1963, 1965, 1977). Such arguments led to demands on state governments to limit the power of physicians to hospitalize individuals. By the beginning of the 21st century, regulations in many countries severely restricted the incarceration of the psychiatrically ill.

Then, because some critics considered ECT, lobotomy, and psychiatric drugs intrusive and brain-damaging, state governments were called upon to limit and proscribe these treatments. As lobotomy (psychosurgery) had already been widely replaced by antipsychotic drugs, the regulations limited lobotomy research but had little direct impact on a practice that had already waned (Valenstein, 1980, 1986). Insulin coma therapy was abandoned when it was shown that the new medications were easier to use, safer, and of almost equal efficacy (Fink et al., 1958; Fink, 2003). Despite studies that showed ECT was more effective than medicines in treating depression, the enthusiasm for medicines quickly replaced ECT in many hospitals and academic centers.

At best, medication reduced the symptoms of severe psychiatric disorders, often leaving enervated and persistently debilitated conditions. By the 1970s, faced with increasing numbers of symptomatic ill, clinicians recalled the use of ECT. In the interim, however, as a by-product of the public challenges to the authority of the state, many legislatures had imposed strict restrictions on ECT practice, limiting the age criteria and the indications (to last resort treatment), and introducing restraining consent requirements. (APA, 1978; Fink, 1991; Shorter, 1997). The image of ECT as an intrusive treatment associated with forced incarceration severely tainted its image.

Disrespect for Privacy

The primitive conditions of many mental hospitals did not encourage respect when treatments were administered. Patients were often poorly clothed. Those who had soiled themselves remained in unpleasant states for hours. All activities took place in large open wards. Restraints, screaming, and assaultive behaviors were commonplace. In this scene of bedlam, treatments were given in the same open wards and with little respect for privacy.

It was under these conditions that ECT was initially given with a mobile ECT device. Overactive and loud-voiced patients who were difficult to control were treated in their beds, barely hidden behind screens. Other patients could not avoid hearing what was going on. These unpleasant experiences were related to friends and relatives, giving ECT the image of a brutal treatment. They were described in the public press, and soon became standard fare in film and television portrayals of psychiatric care (Gabbard & Gabbard, 1987).

Not that ECT was selectively abused. Limb and wet sheet restraints and isolation chambers allowed patients and even visitors to see patients under adverse and unpleasant conditions. Following lobotomies, patients returned to the wards in a stupefied state, with fresh bleeding around their eyes (Freeman et al., 1942; Valenstein, 1980, 1986; Briska, 1997). In insulin coma, secondary episodes of hypoglycemia, seizures, and coma occurred among patients herded together in their ward units (Fink, 2003). These other treatments were abandoned, leaving ECT as the main residual to which the memories of abuse were attached.

Libertarian movements, encouraged by an optimism that the new medications would allow patients to live outside psychiatric hospitals, spawned the drive to de-institutionalization and the emptying of state supported psychiatric hospitals (Isaac & Armat, 1990; Johnson, 1990). Thousands of patients were released to live in the streets and slums of the cities, to fill the prisons, and to become mainstays of the revolving door actions of psychiatric treatment centers rather than being cared for in institutions. Public disgust encouraged a widespread pessimism for all psychiatric treatments including ECT.

ECT as Restraint

Following each seizure, patients are sedated, stuporous, and confused, encouraging its use not as a treatment of an illness but as a means of sedation of unruly patients. Such use was never condoned and often condemned. It was abandoned and was replaced by the intramuscular or intravenous administration of highly potent antipsychotic drugs, especially haloperidol (Okasha & Tewfik, 1964; Rees & Davies, 1965). Although useful as a low dose preparation in the relief of psychosis, haloperidol has often been given in very high doses. Such dosing entailed severe extrapyramidal motor effects, irreversible tardive dyskinesia, and a febrile malignant syndrome. It took another decade for such use to be abandoned, although reports of its use and toxicity persist (Riker et al., 1994; Seneff & Mathews, 1995). Failure to assure informed voluntary consent and coercion at the time of injections are features of this use of antipsychotic drugs. From an ethical point of view, it can be called in question whether ECT and high doses of neuroleptic drugs differ as methods of restraint.

While this image of forced administration of ECT is widely held, in actual practice today, ECT is almost always given to voluntary patients who consent to the treatment.

Confusion among Biological Treatments

Convulsive therapy has been in continuous use for more than 70 years. It was introduced in 1934 and is considered old-fashioned. It is sometimes confused with two other treatments that were introduced concurrently, insulin coma in 1933 and lobotomy in 1935. Since these treatments are now abandoned, it is often a surprise to physicians and families that ECT is still in use. In their testimony about their illnesses and treatment with ECT, Endler (1982), Manning (1994), Rosenberg (2002), and Nuland (2003), among many other observers, each remarks on their surprise when their physicians broached its use (chapter 4).

The treatments have superficial similarities. They were applied in the same populations of patients labeled as suffering from schizophrenia. With increasing experience, they were also applied to patients with manic depressive illness in its depressed and manic forms.

A second commonality is the incidence of grand mal seizures for each of the treatments. Seizures are the therapeutic agent in convulsive therapy, both the pharmaco-convulsive and electroconvulsive forms. Numerous attempts to replace seizures with anesthesia alone or sham seizures failed (Fink, 1979; Palmer, 1980; Abrams, 2002). Seizures occurred in about 10% of insulin coma treatments. When the benefits of the comas alone were not sufficient, electrical-induced seizures were superimposed (Fink, 2003). After frontal lobe surgery, more than half the patients developed spontaneous seizures (National Commission, 1977; Shutts, 1982; Valenstein, 1980, 1986). In retrospect, seizures could be seen as the common element in these interventions, contributing to the efficacy of insulin coma and frontal lobe surgery, as well as being central to convulsive therapy (Fink, 1979, 1993, 2003).

The criteria for selecting one treatment over another were poorly defined, confusing professional and public minds. The blurred distinctions are exemplified by the presentation of ECT and lobotomy in the popular novel and film *One Flew over the Cuckoo's Nest* in which the protagonist undergoes both treatments (Kesey, 1972). In the recent film *A Beautiful Mind* the patient receiving insulin coma is depicted as undergoing a dramatic grand mal seizure (Fink, 2003).

Insulin coma and frontal lobe surgery were poorly effective with high rates of morbidity and mortality. Both were replaced by antipsychotic drugs, but the memory of those experiences still confuses the image of ECT. The psychiatric profession has not been successful in educating the population about the differences among the treatments.

Treatment Properties

Discomfort with Seizures

Both seizures and electricity are repellant features of ECT that encourage unfavorable attitude to its use.

Spontaneous epileptic seizures are frightening and may be associated with injury and death. They have been perceived as blows from the gods, reflecting something evil or sinful. In some cultures epileptic subjects were favored and their statements deemed to be holy, but more often they were considered tainted and badly treated. Many epileptics were ostracized from the community.

Professional attitudes to seizures vary profoundly. At one time, neurologists and psychiatrists were part of a single discipline, comfortable in treating the spontaneous seizures of epilepsy and also in inducing seizures in ECT. With progress in diagnostic methods and increased emphasis on psychoanalysis and psychotherapy, especially in the United States, the disciplines separated. Those who practiced psychoanalysis and psychotherapy became the mainstays of departments of psychiatry and treated the mentally ill in psychiatric and general medical hospitals and offices. Those who focused their interest on structural brain disorders, cerebrospinal fluid examinations, electroencephalography, and brain imaging techniques became the mainstays of departments of neurology and treated their patients in general medical hospitals. The eradication of epilepsy has become their principal focus and their attitude to seizures is uncompromising. Some find it difficult to accept that seizures may be safely induced for therapeutic purposes. Denying such uses, they are unacquainted with the benefits of ECT, exaggerate the risks, and ignore the unique experimental opportunity to study seizures induced in man. Such an attitude does their patients no service.

Fear of Electricity

The widespread fear of electricity strengthens the image of a dangerous and painful procedure. Not that electricity is essential to the benefits of convulsive therapy; it is not, for effective treatments can be given using chemicals, as was the practice when pharmaco-convulsive therapy was first developed (Meduna, 1935, 1937; Fink, 1979).

Images of lightning strikes, of electrocution to end the life of criminals, and reports of the use of electricity in human torture come to mind by the unfortunate name of "electroshock." The discomfort at accepting electricity to be administered in ECT may be contrasted with the unhesitating acceptance of jolts of electricity to the body in electrical cardioversion of a fibrillating heart, seeing this application as a life saving procedure. In the actual practice of ECT, neither the patient nor the spectators experience a shock. For the spectator, cardioversion is much more shocking than modern ECT.

The perception of ECT as one of many electricity-based medical procedures is presented in *Pushbutton Psychiatry* (Kneeland & Warren, 2002). The authors, a historian and a sociologist, see ECT on the boundary between legitimate medicine and quackery. They describe the invention, retrenchment, and resurgence of ECT in American society where the swing of the pendulum of interest has probably been more extensive than in other countries. The initial enthusiasm for ECT was based on the fascination with electricity and with machinery, as well as the early favorable results in severely ill patients. The authors ascribe the decline in ECT use to the phasing-out of large mental hospitals, an impact of patients' rights movements, and the wider use of psychoactive drugs. They see the resurgence of ECT during the last two decades as a disappointment with drug treatment as many patients do not become free of symptoms.

The fear of electricity has strongly influenced the search for alternatives to ECT. Some clinicians now set their hopes on magnetism as safer than electricity. Magnetic stimulation of the brain without inducing seizures, however, has no convincing effects in relieving psychosis or mood disorders (George & Belmaker, 2000; Schlaepfer et al., 2003). Inductions of seizures with magnetic stimulation ("magnetic seizure therapy") may be useful, but the cumbersome nature and the extraordinary expense of the equipment will probably discourage such use (Lisanby et al., 2001; Schlaepfer et al., 2003).

A similar motivation to avoid electricity encouraged Austrian clinicians to suggest anesthesia to achieve prolonged periods of flat EEG brain electrical activity as a replacement for ECT (Langer et al., 1985). The early promise of this method has not been fulfilled and the lack of benefit, expense, and risks discourage its use (Greenberg et al., 1987; Langer et al., 1995).

Implanting a battery-operated nerve stimulator in the chest wall with electrodes connected to the vagus nerve in the neck has recently been hawked as a replacement for ECT (Schachter & Schmidt, 2001; Kosel & Schlaepfer, 2003). This technique is said to augment the anti-epileptic drugs in patients with intractable epilepsy. Its benefits as a replacement for ECT in treating refractory depression have yet to be demonstrated.

None of the substitutes that seek to avoid the anticipated risks of electricity has proved effective. Indeed, these failed experiments support the view that the induction of grand mal seizures is essential to the effects of ECT (Ottosson, 1960, 1986; Fink, 1979, 1999, 2003).

Effects on Memory

It is the effect on memory that is most widely emphasized as so severe as to inhibit the use of ECT for any psychiatric condition. When convulsive therapy was first used, delirious states were elicited for several hours after each treatment. Patients appeared to be in a dream state, poorly responsive to questions, and not spontaneous in their speech or actions. Recollection of the events during, before, and after the treatment course was compromised. Psychologists and psychoanalysts latched on to this effect as an explanation of its mode of action. Basing their views on Freudian theory, they imagined that seizures suppressed memories of childhood trauma that they deemed to be the basis for psychological symptoms (Janis, 1950). To the extent that such suppression served a clinical purpose, they saw ECT as useful. Others complained that the memory effects were compelling evidence that an individual's persona and individuality were altered. They asserted these effects to be permanent and opposed its use (Group for the Advancement of Psychiatry [GAP], 1947).

Modern ECT has come a long way from these origins. Oxygenation, anesthesia, muscle relaxation, modifications in the form and doses of the energies, and variations in electrode placements have reduced the immediate cognitive effects, making the treatments more tolerable. Electrical stimulation, seizures, and anesthesia still impact on recollection but the effects are of short duration. A persistent inability to remember the chaotic days of severe illness is a feature of the illness and is usually independent of whether ECT is given or not. Only occasionally do patients experience long-lasting retrograde and anterograde amnesia. Even in such cases, the role of ECT is uncertain.

Credible evidence for persistent brain effects in modern treatment is lacking. Animal studies fail to find changes in brain structure despite intensive treatment schedules. Instead, neurogenesis is enhanced by seizures (Madsen et al., 2000a, b; Wennström et al., 2004)

Ideological Factors

Antipsychiatry

The frail base of clinical evidence and the lack of impartial public information about ECT gave free rein to imagination and ideology. Antipsychiatry movements sprang up after the Second World War and quickly found ECT as a susceptible target (Fink, 1991; Shorter, 1997; Abrams, 2002; Ottosson, 2003). Attacks on the role and functions of psychiatrists were sanctioned by such influential political writers as Thomas Szasz (1961) and Kenneth Kesey (1962) in the United States, Ronald Laing (1960, 1976) in Great Britain, Franco Basaglia (1968, 1987) in Italy, and Michael Foucault (1965) in France. To the extent that their criticism was leveled at unacceptable conditions in large state mental hospitals, it was justified. It was exaggerated, however, by popularizing the belief that mental illness was a myth, engendered by the state to exert control over its nonconforming citizens. They argued that psychotic patients were following individual drummers and that the state had no right or responsibility to marshal their unique thoughts or attitudes in its service or to proscribe them. They saw the state's acquiescence in psychosurgery, ECT, and forced sterilization of patients as reprehensible and indistinguishable from the actions against special populations in Nazi Germany, fascist Italy, and communist Russia (Szasz, 1961, 1963, 1965, 1977).

Former patients mounted attacks on ECT in the belief that they had been harmed by the care that they had received. Organized lay groups sought to ban the use of ECT by legislation and to encourage patients to charge their physicians with malpractice. In the United States these groups take on the names of "Citizens against Psychiatric Assault" (www.psychassault.org), the "Committee for Truth in Psychiatry" (www.harborside. com/~equinox/ect.htm), and the "Citizen's Commission on Human Rights" (www.cchr.org). The CCHR was founded in 1969 by the Church of Scientology and Dr. Thomas Szasz. Since then, the website asserts, it has grown to 133 chapters in 34 countries. Each group attracts members by calling on them to defend individuals against the powers of medicine. They are supported by a small coterie of professionals.

The Church of Scientology is a large and well-funded faith-based membership organization led by lay preachers (Hubbard, 1951; Church, 1992). It directs the members' ire against psychiatric practices, especially ECT, psychosurgery, and the use of psychotropic drugs in children and adolescents. These groups harass legislative committees, disturb public mental health meetings, and intimidate speakers at scientific sessions. In the United States, they are frequent speakers on radio and television talk-shows where the hosts encourage a circus atmosphere rather than reasoned discourse.

The same citizens entreated the U.S. Food and Drug Administration (FDA) to review the classification of ECT devices, seeking a classification that would require extensive documentation of efficacy before approval for sale (Abrams, 2002). The FDA recommended the reclassification in 1978 and approached the problem anew in 1990, proposing a definitive rule to limit the application of ECT devices to treatment of depressive disorders alone. After actions by the U.S. Congress, this rule was not established. The only effect of these machinations has been an FDA regulation to limit the energy output of devices sold in the United States. This limitation impinges on the ability of clinicians to adequately treat patients with high seizure thresholds and is an unreasonable impediment to good medical practice (Sackeim, 1991; Abrams, 2000; Krystal et al., 2000).

Antipathy within Psychiatry

Even among psychiatrists, the schism has been broad and resistance to ECT widespread. In the period immediately after the Second World War, protagonists of psychodynamic theories sought and successfully achieved control of American psychiatry (Fink, 1979, 1991, 1999; Isaac & Armat, 1990; Grob, 1994; Hale, 1995). They viewed psychiatric illnesses as the result of unconscious conflicts and declared their views with the fervor of religious conviction. These views contrasted strongly with the biological-minded psychiatrists who saw the illnesses as consequences of brain dysfunction and disease. Some psychodynamic-oriented psychiatrists regarded biological treatments as assaults on the brain and disparaged practitioners for such use (Breggin, 1979; Szasz, 1961, 1963, 1977; Morgan, 1985).

Convulsive therapy is a complex treatment that requires anesthesia and the laying on of the hands. It differs markedly from the passive posture set as a standard for the dynamic psychotherapies. The touching of patients is antithetic to psychodynamic principles; the practice bars physical contact between patient and therapist. Also, ECT requires technical skills that are not part of conventional psychiatric practice, widening the gap in thinking and practice among practitioners. Modern psychiatric diagnoses are descriptive, not based on objective criteria. They demarcate syndromes poorly. In the confusion of unspecific psychiatric diagnoses and the turbulence of hawked treatments, new competition for patients ensues between the specialists of both camps, especially in the United States. The competition was particularly strong immediately after the Second World War when the psychoanalysts established the politically active group for the advancement of psychiatry (GAP) that openly attacked the use of ECT (Fink, 1979, 1991, 1997). The competition muted as psychiatric practice was increasingly dominated by psychopharmacology. As practitioners devoted more and more of their energies to medication treatments, the same competition persisted, only now between ECT on one hand and medication or psychotherapies on the other.

The fully trained psychiatrist is expected to offer the most effective treatment for a patient's illness. Evidence-based medicine is increasingly a feature of modern health care. For a number of psychiatric illnesses, ECT is the most effective treatment. The limited experience with ECT among American psychiatrists makes it difficult for many patients to receive the most effective treatment (Hermann et al., 1998). The impact is seen in the population of patients referred for ECT. They are mainly those who have failed multiple trials of medications and psychotherapy and have been ill for many months, even years (Mulsant et al., 1997; Olfson et al., 1998; Petrides et al., 2001).

Another factor in the antipathy to the use of ECT is the impact of the pharmaceutical industry on clinical trials. Industry funding dominates the assessment of new psychotropic drugs, defraying the costs of clinical trials by consulting fees to the practitioners and full reimbursement of the expenses. They design the studies, analyze the results, and at times, write the reports for investigators' signature (Healy, 1997, 2002, 2003; Relman & Angell, 2002; Als-Nielsen et al., 2003; Moynihan, 2003; Healy & Thase, 2003).

The education of psychiatrists in postgraduate training programs is dominated by industry funding. At one time, the expenses for travel and honoraria for academic teachers were defrayed by the hospitals and academic centers, underwritten by grants from the National Institutes of Health. The programs ended in the United States when reductions in the federal budget were required by the excesses of the Vietnam War. Increasingly, the support of academic activities has been undertaken by the pharmaceutical industry. Companies fund weekly grand rounds and journal club meetings at hospitals, lectures at national and international meetings, travel costs and attendance fees for the participants in large psychiatric meetings, and extensive advertising in medical journals. More than half the attendees and almost all the lecturers at meetings of the American Psychiatric Association and World Psychiatric Association and similar sessions are selected by local industry representatives who defray expenses of travel and participation. The practitioners and teachers who are selected support the role of new drugs in the care of their patients. While the domination is most flagrant in the United States, it is a feature of medical practice throughout the world. If ECT is touched upon at all, it is pictured as a competitor to the drugs and even when its use would be appropriate, as in depressed, manic, and psychotic patients who have failed medication trials, its study and the teaching of its role is neglected. The same lecturers selected by industry are the experts who make up the treatment algorithms for the principal psychiatric conditions in which ECT is generally cited as a treatment of last resort or after the three or more failed trials of the latest introduced medications (Healy, 1997, 2002, 2003).

Economic Factors

Conventional economic factors stigmatize the treatment. Despite the complexity of ECT in requiring a treatment team and well-equipped facilities, fees for the treatments are low, making it economically difficult for practitioners to offer the service. Legislative restraints force families to call on lawyers and the courts to assure permission for the treatment. Such services are daunting and expensive. Special governmental reporting requirements, not features of conventional medical practice, are additional costs in its use. ECT practitioners are harassed by malpractice claims and public ignominy by inclusion on published lists that ridicule the practice. In some venues, economic factors limit the use of anesthesia, either by a dearth of anesthesiologists or the expense of the medications. The lack of adequate facilities for anesthesia forces physicians to the unfortunate choice of unmodified ECT with its risks or not to administer ECT and not to offer the patient effective relief.

Professional Counteractions

The attacks on ECT have not gone undefended. The American Psychiatric Association established a Task Force on Electroconvulsive Therapy in 1975. Its 1978 report summarized the evidence for the use of ECT in the treatment of major depressions, intractable mania, and therapy-resistant schizophrenia (APA, 1978). It recommended guidelines for signed voluntary consent in psychiatric practice, encouraging a less authoritarian approach, full disclosure of the prospects and risks of treatment, and urged that patients be free to discontinue treatment at any time. The British Royal College of Psychiatrists next surveyed the practice, reported similar indications, and made similar recommendations for practice and consent (Pippard & Ellam, 1981). They found that one-third of the practitioners administered ECT poorly and that more than half the facilities were ill-equipped. These revelations brought a stinging rebuke from the editors of *The Lancet* (Editor, 1981).

Awareness that American patients were subject to the same risks led to the widespread adoption of the 1978 American Psychiatric Association report as a hospital standard and its use as the guidelines for care in court proceedings. In 1985, a Consensus Conference under the combined auspices of the National Institutes of Health (NIH) and of Mental Health (NIMH) concluded that ECT was an effective treatment for specific mental illnesses, its practice was safe, and that interdiction was not warranted (Consensus Conference, 1985).

The 1978 recommendations were upgraded in 1990 and again in 2001, leaving intact the guidelines for voluntary signed consent (APA, 1990, 2001). Similar guidelines for ECT have been developed by national commissions and societies in Canada, Australia, Denmark, Great Britain, and the Netherlands, and endorsed in individual texts in other nations.

The turmoil has had some favorable effects on psychiatric practice. Based on clinical experience of ECT and gratitude from successfully treated patients, the positive effects of ECT are described in the Task Force reports in the United States and Great Britain and in texts (Fink, 1979; Palmer, 1981; Abrams & Essman, 1982; Fraser, 1982; Kalinowsky, Hippius & Klein, 1982; Taylor, Sierles & Abrams, 1985; Malitz & Sackeim, 1986; Abrams, 1988; Endler & Persad, 1988; Kiloh, Smith & Johnson, 1988). New educational videotapes facilitate informed consent (*Somatics*, 1986a, b; Grunhaus & Barroso, 1989). There has been a marked increase in journal articles on ECT, the formation of a journal dedicated to convulsive therapy in 1985 (*Convulsive Therapy*, now *Journal of ECT*), as well as a national society dedicated to the treatment (Association for Convulsive Therapy). Educational courses to improve the skills of practitioners have been developed and hospitals have adopted the APA reports as their standard for practice. A greater alliance between psychiatrists and anesthesiologists has encouraged treatment teams competent to manage the most severe medically ill patient for whom ECT is a life-saving consideration (Abrams, 1989).

The negative effects, however, are more prominent. ECT is taught in a limited number of medical schools and residency training sites. Because of restricted interest and availability, psychiatrists who wish to use ECT in their practice depend on postgraduate education courses (continuing medical education) or apprenticeships outside their residency training for practical experience. In the United States, ECT is largely ignored by state, federal, and municipal psychiatric hospitals where the majority of the severe psychiatrically ill, the principal candidates for ECT, are treated. The picture, however, is not as dark everywhere. In the Scandinavian countries ECT is given in hospitals and on an out-patient basis on equal footing with drugs and psychotherapy.

The stigma of ECT has severely impeded research into its mechanisms of action. The psychiatrists who are interested in ECT find it difficult to obtain approval for experimental studies and almost impossible to obtain financial support from governmental or private funding sources. The few studies in the United States that have been financed by public agencies are technical in nature and almost none have been directed to understanding its mechanism of action. In the past decade, the NIMH has supported studies of continuation medications after unilateral ECT and a comparison of continuation with ECT or with medication, both as multisite studies in unipolar depressed patients. A direct comparison of three electrode placements in depressed patients is underway in a multisite study, and ECT augmentation of clozapine in psychosis rounds out the list of major studies.

National Assessments

Numerous assessments of ECT have been made by commissions, some organized by governmental bodies, others by national societies, and still others by self-appointed expert committees. Each assessment seeks a balanced image of the efficacy and safety of ECT, based in part on the published literature, and often on the self reports of disaffected patients. Some commissions are called together in response to legal challenges; at times, their work has resulted in legislation that proscribed and limited the use of ECT. In the past year, the Indian Supreme Court has been asked to prohibit unmodified treatment, a form that is still in use in developing countries because of the expense of anesthesia and the dearth of trained anesthesiologists (Mudur, 2003; Andrade et al., 2003).

In early 2003, in response to demands by lay groups that ECT should be banned, the British National Institute for Clinical Excellence, a governmental body empowered to evaluate medical treatments, assessed the merits of electroconvulsive treatment. (NICE 2003) The NICE report recommended

> ... that electroconvulsive therapy is used only to achieve rapid and short term improvement of severe symptoms, after an adequate trial of other treatment options has proven ineffective and/or when the condition is considered to be potentially life threatening, in individuals with severe depressive illness, catatonia, [and] a prolonged or severe manic episode. (p. 5)

The report considers maintenance ECT as unproven, and finds no role for ECT in schizophrenia and mania. It is more restrictive than the 1989 U.K. report of the Royal College of Psychiatrists and the more recent Scottish ECT Audit Network (Freeman et al., 2000; SEAN, 2002).

A supporting commentary on the NICE report seeks to allay the fears of the report's instigators by predicting: *"... that most parties will be reasonably satisfied with the NICE appraisal. Those concerned about potential overuse of the treatment can be reassured with the restrictions, increased safeguards, and improved consent procedures"* (Carney & Geddes, 2003, p. 1544).

To bolster the NICE report, an essay by Rose et al. (2003) was requested by the NICE commission and then praised by Carney and Geddes (2003). The NICE report brought letters of criticism that argued that the report was too restrictive and inconsistent with the guidelines for ECT of the Royal College of Psychiatrists (Evans et al., 2003; Cole & Tobiansky, 2003).

The national specialist societies in United Kingdom do not agree that ECT should be reserved for treatment-resistant and severe depression that has failed prior medication trials. For some conditions, ECT is a primary treatment. The evidence base for the benefit of ECT in moderately severe depression is also strong (U.K. ECT Review Group, 2003).

Patient choice is another basis for ECT. A patient should be free to choose ECT over other treatment alternatives. It is perverse that patients, having had a good response to ECT and knowing from previous experience that it will relieve their depressive symptoms when antidepressants may not, should have to wait until their depression becomes severe or fails to respond to other treatments before they can receive ECT. The SEAN (2002) report finds patient choice associated with one of the best response rates to ECT.

While we lack randomized controlled trials to support continuation (maintenance) ECT, there is sufficient evidence from clinical experience that the remission associated with ECT in some patients cannot be sustained by lithium, antidepressants, or psychotherapy or their combinations, and that the patients can only stay well when continuation ECT is used (Fink et al., 1996; Gagne et al., 2000).

The societies consider ECT as a treatment of first choice when the patient chooses the treatment because of previous good response, is in a psychotic depressive disorder that is extremely unlikely to respond to other treatments such as psychotherapy or antidepressants, in a depressive stupor, or exhibiting such severe retardation as to be at risk of death.

A more generous view towards ECT is also shown by a Canadian agency with the responsibility to assess medical treatments in the province of Quebec (AETMIS, 2003). Noting the controversial nature of ECT and the resurgence of its use, the report states that the incidence in Quebec is similar to that in other industrialized countries. The report concludes:

> We have excellent evidence that ECT is indicated for major depression.... In the opinion of experts, ECT appears to act more quickly and to be more effective than pharmacotherapy.... ECT must therefore be considered to be an accepted technology for the following indications:
>
>> cases of severe major depression presenting resistance or intolerance to pharmacotherapy for which cognitive psychotherapy is not indicated or has not had any therapeutic effect;
>>
>> patients presenting a high suicide risk; and
>>
>> patients presenting psychic suffering or marked physical deterioration requiring very rapid onset of therapeutic action. (p. viii)

The commission recommends increased funding for studies of ECT, the registration of treatments, the developments of more specific guidelines for its use, and specifically asks that

> community mental-health groups be given the means to inform patients and the public regarding the evidence concerning ECT and to support patients, their families and friends in the treatment process. (p. x)

Summary

As with all treatments, ECT developed from early trials with failures and complications to its present state of technical refinement, useful indications, and more favorable benefit-to-risk ratios. For most treatments, the difficulties, severe side effects, and even fatalities are accepted as the price of the discovery and the development. ECT, however, although it has undergone a favorable evolution, still carries the burden of complaints of early misuse, neglect of informed consent, association with forced incarceration, and fear of electricity and epileptic seizures. Despite its acknowledged usefulness in the treatment of the severe mentally ill, ECT is so stigmatized that its use is severely restricted and its merits denied. Although the reasons are mainly ideological and not based on science or clinical experience, the attacks have received political attention that has led to legislative restrictions. Despite severe stumbling blocks, practitioners who are faced with the responsibility for the care of individual patients increasingly turn to its use. The fact that an effective and safe treatment is being denied to seriously ill patients for unscientific reasons is a challenge to the ethical principles of medical care.

CHAPTER 2

Principles of Medical Ethics

Gross violations of human rights and human dignity in the experiments on concentration camp prisoners in Germany and the abuse of psychiatric treatments for dissidents in the Soviet Union and China encouraged the development of guiding principles of ethical medical conduct. For clinical research, the codes are the Nuremberg Code of 1947 (Shuster, 1998) and the Declaration of Helsinki of 1964, amended several times, the latest in Washington, D.C. in 2002 (World Medical Association, 2000, 2002). For psychiatric care, the codes are the Declaration of Hawaii of 1977 (World Psychiatric Association [WPA], 1978) and the supplementary Declaration of Madrid of 1996 (WPA, 2003). The codes encourage the continuing evaluation of medical treatment and research as to their conformity with ethical principles and with the scientific evidence of efficacy and safety.

Core Principles of Ethics

Principles of Biomedical Ethics, a seminal work that first appeared in 1979, endorsed four principles of ethics (Beauchamp & Childress, 2001). Without ranking their importance, the principles are beneficence (doing good), non-maleficence (not doing harm), autonomy (respect for the individual), and justice (being fair). These principles are sometimes referred to as the "Georgetown mantra" since the authors are faculty members at Georgetown University in Washington, D.C. Good reasons merit the support of these principles as action guides in clinical work.

The U.S. Institute of Medicine proposed six consistent principles in the design of a health care system (Institute of Medicine, 2001). The services must be:

safe—avoid injuries from care that is intended to help;

effective—provide services based on scientific knowledge to all who can benefit and to withhold services for those not likely to benefit. Seriously ill persons must not be deprived of all hope of improvement or recovery of function;

patient-centered—provide care that is respectful and responsive to individual patient preferences, needs, and values;

timely—reduce wait and sometimes harmful delays for both those who receive and those who give care;

efficient—avoid waste; and,

equitable—provide care that does not vary in quality because of patient characteristics such as gender, ethnicity, geography, or socioeconomic status.

Care should also be based "*on a continuous healing relationship.*" In the care of the psychiatrically ill, the lack of continuing relationships is particularly acute. In-patient and out-patient care is generally fractionated and continuing healing relationships are not encouraged for many, if not most, of those who need care and treatment.

These guidelines augment the Georgetown principles with demands for timeliness, efficiency, and continuity.

The World Health Organization (1996) has endorsed ten basic principles for mental health care law that are consistent with the Georgetown principles. They add self-determination, a right to be assisted in self-determination, opportunity for the least restrictive alternative, and availability of review procedures.

Principle of Beneficence

The goal of health care is to promote the welfare of each patient—sometimes to cure, often to alleviate, and always to comfort. Patients are entitled to the opportunity for relief from illness, an obligation that is accepted by health care workers with the promise that they will offer the best care according to evidence-based medicine. Medical measures are to be based on clinical science and not on prejudice, superstition, tradition, or political correctness. When two or more interventions are available, patients should be offered the most effective.

Triage, the sorting of patients for health care, is a necessary feature when health care facilities are not able to support optimal treatment for all patients. The urgency of a patient's needs and prospects for successful treatment are compelling considerations.

Concerning the allocation of public resources, a Swedish Parliamentary Priorities Commission proposed highest priority to

> care of life-threatening acute diseases and diseases that, if left untreated, will lead to permanent disability or premature death.

The same high priority is to be given to

> treatment of severe chronic diseases, palliative terminal care, and care of people with reduced autonomy.

Applied to mental health care, these principles offer the highest priority to those with psychoses who are involuntarily committed to hospital, depressive patients at suicidal risk, patients with chronic psychoses and depressive-anxiety states, and those who, because of reduced autonomy, cannot assert their rights. The latter group includes the demented and mentally retarded (Swedish Parliamentary Priorities Commission, 1995).

An American Psychiatric Association "Vision for the Mental Health System" underscores the needs of the severely and persistently mentally ill, including among other things

> Full access to treatment, rehabilitation, and support services in a coordinated and comprehensive system of care that is culturally competent (APA, 2003, p. 4).

Other needs are continuity of care, treatment supported by the best research evidence, and treatment in the least restrictive setting consistent with safety and reasonable expectations of benefit.

Based on its high prevalence rate and associated disability, major depression is presented as a leading cause of disability in the United States. Bipolar disorder and schizophrenia are also cited as disorders with high prevalence and high morbidity that contribute to years of disability.

> In the United States the burden for disease accounted for by mental disorders is 20 percent, whereas only 5 to 7 percent of all health expenditures are directed toward treatment of these disorders. (p. 7)

The report also states:

> Medicare continues to discriminate against treatment for mental illness by requiring 50 percent co-pay for psychiatrists in contrast to a 20 percent co-pay for other physicians. Parity for mental health care under Medicare is a long overdue and urgent priority (APA, 2003, p. 6).

The priority settings of the American Psychiatric Association (2003) and the Swedish Parliamentary Priorities Commission (1995) are in close agreement.

Since need is best seen in relation to benefit, an individual can only need that which is beneficial. In the management of severe depression, especially in patients with a risk of suicide, the most effective relief comes from early intervention. It is wasteful (and riskful) to offer treatments that promise partial relief and fail to offer a treatment that has a possibility of full relief.

Treatment options vary in efficacy and cost. To utilize public and individual health care resources in the most responsible way, health care seeks a reasonable relationship between cost and benefit. Treatments that offer high efficacy at low cost are to be preferred over those with low efficacy and high cost. When patients are informed of the risks and benefits of treatments, the direct and indirect costs are necessary parts of the picture. For example, two treatments may eventually lead to full relief of symptoms, but the one that is slower in effect implies a longer time spent ill, loss of work income, and the extra costs of hospital and home care. How much additional cost is acceptable in pursuit of a desired outcome?

Principle of Nonmaleficence

The Hippocratic axiom *primum non nocere* (above all, do no harm) combines the principles of beneficence and nonmaleficence: *"I will use treatment to help the sick according to my ability and judgment, but I will never use it to injure or wrong them."*

Even if we consider it self-evident that psychiatry, as all of medicine, aims at doing good and not harm, we acknowledge that no effective treatment is so safe as to only do good. Every intervention carries risks, many that are well known as well as those that are unintended. At the same time that antipsychotic drugs relieve hallucinations and delusions, they may induce tiredness, feelings of alienation, and movement disorders. Before antidepressant drugs have elevated the depressive mood, they may increase anxiety, increase suicide risk, and elicit sexual dysfunctions. The most known and feared side effect of ECT is impaired memory.

In recommending an intervention, the clinician considers the balance of benefits and risks; a favorable benefit-to-risk ratio is an indispensable strength of any treatment.

Respect for Autonomy

Respect for autonomy and personal integrity is a dominating theme of codes of ethics. The principles of psychiatric ethics were drawn up by the Swedish psychiatrist and ethicist Clarence Blomquist while holding a scholarship at the Hastings Center in New York (Blomquist, 1977; Ottosson, 2000). These were codified in the Hawaii Declaration, and adopted by acclamation by the General Assembly of the World Psychiatric Association in 1977. The Declaration formulated the conditions for involuntary care and proscribed the use of psychiatry in diagnosis, classification, or treatment for political purposes in the absence of a defined psychiatric illness. Guideline 5 states that:

> No procedure shall be performed nor treatment given against or independent of a patient's own will, unless because of mental illness, the patient cannot form a judgment as to what is in his or her own best interest and without which treatment serious impairment is likely to occur to the patient or others.

Guideline 7 reads:

> The psychiatrist must never use his professional possibilities to violate the dignity or human rights of any individual or group and should never let inappropriate personal desires, feelings, prejudices or beliefs interfere with the treatment. The psychiatrist must on no account utilize the tools of his profession, once the absence of psychiatric illness has been established. If a patient or some third party demands actions contrary to scientific knowledge or ethical principles the psychiatrist must refuse to cooperate.

The Declaration of Madrid is an amplification of the Declaration of Hawaii and has restrictive guidelines on the participation of psychiatrists in euthanasia, torture, sex selection, and organ transplantation. Later guidelines on psychiatry addressing the media, discrimination on ethnic or cultural grounds, genetic research, psychotherapy, conflict of interest with the industry, conflict with third party payers, and violating the clinical boundaries are scheduled to be considered by the World Psychiatric Association General Assembly at a future meeting (Okasha, 2003).

Both the Declaration of Hawaii and that of Madrid emphasize the responsibility of psychiatrists to develop treatments that minimally restrict the freedom of patients and that enable an equitable distribution of healthcare resources. The codes encourage psychiatrists to be familiar with scientific developments in psychiatry and acknowledge the right of patients to make voluntary and informed decisions based on mutual trust and respect. They call upon psychiatrists to inform patients about their illness and what is known about its causes and its relief so that they can make rational decisions according to their personal values and preferences (Say & Thomson, 2003).

Individual autonomy is based on voluntary choice and independence of forced actions. An autonomous choice is one that is made with an understanding of the consequences of the decision and without outside controlling influences. Autonomy encompasses more than informed consent, acceptance or refusal of treatment, and choice in decision-making. As the distribution of knowledge between health care professionals and patients is unequal, professionals have the obligation to fully disclose the information that will insure the patient's comprehension of the consequences of both accepting and of refusing a recommended intervention. The clinician is obliged to present adequate information in a manner that is understandable by the individual, with due regard to the patient's education and comprehension. Without an explanation and consideration of the consequences of a decision for or against an intervention, consent or refusal cannot be considered informed. Patients who are ignorant, sick, frightened, or inexperienced are a challenge to the communication skills and the patience of clinicians.

An individual's competence in decision making may be adequate for many aspects of life, but in a clinical context, the crucial capacity is the ability to understand what is recommended and how it achieves the best outcome. Psychiatric illnesses, however, often distort comprehension so that no explanation of risks and benefits enables an autonomous decision (Matthews, 2000). For patients who lack the ability to make a valid decision, the psychiatrist is obliged to seek an alternative consent from the family, to apply for judicial authorization, or to make the necessary immediate decisions respecting the dignity and legal rights of the patients.

We expect autonomous individuals to have the right to accept or to refuse treatment. Those individuals who are not autonomous and no longer can decide still deserve to receive effective treatment. We are in sympathy with the concept of "weak paternalism" (Beauchamp & Childress, 2001). When patients exhibit compromised ability, physicians are encouraged to act as responsible parents towards their children. It would be callous and uncaring not to treat an illness that substantially reduces a person's choices and actions (Merskey, 1999). The assumption of responsibility by paternalism, however, does not substitute for individual consent in the long-term perspective. If utilized, the assumption of responsibility should last no longer than the period of reduced capacity. Paternalism that overrides informed and voluntary decisions by competent patients is not ethical.

Especially when life is in jeopardy, it may be morally defensible for the clinician to assume responsibility for decision making and to override the autonomy of the patient. It may even be morally indefensible not to assume responsibility. In the absence of risk to life or for long-lasting disability, however, no treatment is to be given against the patients' will.

Coercion is to be avoided. If the intervention would clearly be of material benefit and persuasion is unsuccessful, however, it would be wrong not to make an unpopular decision and to yield to the patient's protests.

Confidentiality of information is essential to psychiatric practice. Professional secrecy must not be broken. An exception is to be considered if the patient or a third party would be seriously damaged, physically or mentally, by maintaining secrecy when the release of information can save a life.

Since psychiatric patients are particularly vulnerable, special precautions need be taken to respect their autonomy and integrity in research. Research in psychotic patients who may not be aware of their illness represents an ethical dilemma. On one hand, it may be difficult to assert that a valid consent has been given, on the other more knowledge is needed of such illnesses.

With increasing maturity children must take part in medical decisions, although they have not reached lawful age.

Principle of Justice

Human dignity holds a central position in society's view of justice. The humanistic tradition of the great religions identifies individual dignity as central to ethical behavior, arguing that all individuals have the same rights and are entitled to personal respect. Human dignity is not defined or circumscribed by personal qualities or functions in the community, such as physical or mental ability, social status, gender, occupation, income, or health status, but is inherent in the individual's existence as a human being.

This principle of individual dignity is emphatically stated in Article 1 of the UN Declaration of Human Rights:

> All human beings are born free and equal in dignity and rights. They are endowed with reason and conscience and should act towards one another in a spirit of brotherhood. (United Nations General Assembly, 1948).

Distinctions in a democratic society based on race, color, gender, language, religion, political opinion, national or social origin, property, or social status are unacceptable as described in Article 2. The text emphasizes that the equality of human dignity applies to each individual without exception.

In applying this principle to the treatment of psychiatric illnesses, we find the distribution of health care to be unequal across national boundaries, within states and cities, and even among hospitals according to the economic section of the population that they serve. Such distributive anomalies do not comply with the principle of justice.

Formal justice means that persons with the same illness are to be treated similarly, despite differences in social, economic, or educational status. All persons are eligible for the optimal treatment for their condition. The principle may be difficult to apply when resources are limited, but every effort is to be made to foster its worldwide application.

While most observers concur in formal justice, they differ in distributive justice, that is, how resources should be allocated. Should each person have an equal share of available resources (for instance, access to health care) or should the allocation be done according to individual need, benefit, effort, contribution, merit, social status, or demand in a free market? Beauchamp and Childress (2001) offer alternative approaches to justice according to egalitarian, libertarian, and utilitarian theories. Each has been skillfully defended and advanced to determine how goods and services should be distributed.

Egalitarian theories emphasize equal access to the goods in life that every rational person desires. Libertarian theories emphasize rights to social and economic liberty, while utilitarian principles maximize public utility.

It is impossible to establish a national health care system that fully complies with these principles. Rather, health policy is based on a patchwork of different principles with varying foci.

Libertarian principles in the United States justify the faith that health care is best left to the market place, encouraging competition for patients among doctors and hospitals. Health care is privately and voluntarily purchased by individual initiative except for the elderly and the disabled, for whom a national Medicare system provides support, and the acknowledged poor, for whom an individual state Medicaid system offers health care. In its extreme form U.S. health care is based on demands in the population. Demands may reflect needs but may also be governed by advertising and campaigns which, without scientific reasons, may upgrade or downgrade certain treatments. The pharmaceutical industry plays a decisive role in supporting intensive advertising for their products not only to the health care providers, but directly to the public. In the long perspective, health care on demand will benefit neither the population nor an optimal resource allocation.

In socialist countries, among them Sweden and several countries in Europe, health care is based on a mixture of utilitarian and egalitarian principles. Each member of society, irrespective of wealth or position, is provided with equal access to an adequate (even if not maximal) level of health care. Resources are distributed on the basis of needs, either expressed as demands or following surveys of the state of health in the population. The costs are defrayed through taxation, although patients may pay supplementary fees. Better services, such as luxury hospital rooms, are available for purchase at personal expense or covered by insurance. When dwindling resources have necessitated cost containment, the utilitarian principle has yielded to priority setting where those who are genuinely needy get preference before those with lesser need. In many countries, private or insurance supported care coexists with public care.

Severe mentally ill persons run the risk of not obtaining appropriate care in a libertarian system. Societal support based on the egalitarian system is necessary, though not always sufficient.

We are pessimistic about the possibility of finding a synthesis between these principles for psychiatric care. Like Beauchamp and Childress (2001) we do, however, endorse a rule for fair opportunity that offers a larger distributional share of treatment resources to persons disadvantaged by their disabilities. Special attention needs to be paid to those who are unaware of their human dignity and who have less chance than others of making their voices heard or exercising their rights. People with serious psychiatric illnesses belong to these groups. A policy that insures adequate care is in agreement with respect for human dignity.

Prima Facie Binding

The core principles of medical ethics provide a framework of moral theory for the identification, analysis, and resolution of moral problems in health care. Each is binding as long as it is not overridden by competing principles. In a specific clinical situation, the principles are weighed and the consequences analyzed in both the short and the long-term perspectives. If one principle warrants priority over the others, be it beneficence or respect for autonomy, it is a morally justified infringement and not a morally unjustified violation.

Research Ethics

There may be no medical field in which the limited effectiveness of available treatments generates more persistent despair among patients, their families, and physicians than mental illness. This despair is particurlarly evident with respect to conditions that radically compromise their victims' ability to function successfully in the world, to be themselves, and to enjoy the sense of safety and stability that most people take for granted (Capron, 1999).

The sense of desperation paves the way for clinical research that can create the knowledge to provide relief based on scientific evidence.

A most vexing ethical problem concerns patients with reduced capacity to consent to their participation in research. The Nuremberg Code, formulated in 1947 in response to the trial of Nazi physicians who had experimented on concentration camp prisoners without their consent, stated that "the voluntary consent of the human subject is absolutely essential" (Michels, 1999). The struggle with this ethical dilemma is ongoing. On the one hand, research on human subjects requires informed consent; but, on the other hand, how best to assure consent from those who suffer from impaired decision-making capacity? The Declaration of Helsinki of the World Medical Association softened the absolute ban of the Nuremberg code by allowing legal guardians of incompetent persons to make decisions on their behalf. Paragraph 24 of the Edinburgh revision of the Helsinki Declaration from 2000 reads:

> For a research subject who is legally incompetent, physically or mentally incapable of giving consent or is a legally incompetent minor, the investigator must obtain informed consent from the legally authorized representative in accordance with applicable law. These groups should not be included in research unless the research is necessary to promote the health of the population represented and this research cannot instead be performed on legally competent persons.

The latter point is further emphasized in paragraph 26 prescribing:

> Research on individuals from whom it is not possible to obtain consent, including proxy or advance consent, should be done only if the physical/mental condition that prevents obtaining informed consent is a necessary characteristic of the population.

Most developed countries have institutional review boards or ethics committees to protect the rights of vulnerable populations, including the mentally disabled. In the United States, a commission has offered detailed formal procedures to safeguard the rights of persons with mental disorders that may affect decision-making capacity (National Bioethics Advisory Commission, 1998). Deliberations are ongoing on solutions that will protect persons (not only the mentally disordered) who have impaired decision-making capacity. It is a matter of finding a trade-off among three undesirable events: further stigmatizing the mentally ill, undermining the research agenda for mental illness, and diluting the moral responsibility of researchers (Michels, 1999; Oldham et al., 1999a; Charney, 1999; Childress & Shapiro, 1999; Miller & Fins, 1999; Oldham et al., 1999b).

The latest revision of the Helsinki Declaration also introduces a new aspect on the use of placebo. Paragraph 29 reads:

The benefits, risks, burdens and effectiveness of a new method should be
tested against those of the best current prophylactic, diagnostic, and therapeutic metods. This does not exclude the use of placebo, or no treatment,
in studies where no proven prophylactic, diagnostic or therapeutic method
exists.

The other side of this coin is that the use of placebo is inappropriate when
proven methods exist that can be compared with new treatments with potential advantages over the old ones. Every patient has the right to obtain the
best available treatment.

In a good patient-doctor relationship, most patients, even those with psychotic illnesses, are capable of giving their informed consent to treatment,
and no special measures must be taken. However, it may be less difficult to
get consent for a treatment than explaining, making patients understand, and
accepting a randomized controlled trial. Since the accomplishment of clinical trials can not be a reason for involuntary commitment, certain limitations
on the realization of trials must be accepted in some patient groups.

Summary

Codes of ethical conduct for health care were developed after the Second
World War. They are codified in the Helsinki declaration for clinical research
and the Declarations of Hawaii and Madrid for psychiatric care. Four basic
principles were elaborated for health care: beneficence (doing good), non-
maleficence (not doing harm), autonomy (respect for the individual), and
justice (being fair). Medical measures need to comply with all the principles,
but if that is not possible, an order of priority is established and a choice of
action is made considering the consequences of the various alternatives.

CHAPTER 3

Previous Ethical Approaches to Electroconvulsive Therapy

When convulsive therapy was introduced in the 1930s, the mentally ill were considered incapable of making decisions as to their treatment and care. Their admission to hospital was mostly involuntary, accomplished by certification by a physician. Treatment decisions were made by the hospital authorities. Sedation, convulsive therapy, insulin coma, psychosurgery, and physical restraint were the main treatments for their illnesses. These were applied without consideration of the patient's wishes. Many patients rightfully complained that they had been incarcerated and treated without their consent.

As an example, we cite the suit entered by Austrian soldiers at the end of the First World War against Julius Wagner-Jauregg of the University of Vienna, chief of psychiatry for the Austro-Hungarian Army. Men who had suffered hysterical paralyses and sensory losses had been treated with painful faradic currents. The treatments were ordered and consent was not requested. The principal expert for the plaintiffs, Sigmund Freud, offered opinions that better methods of treatment had been available, citing psychoanalysis, and that faradic currents were punishment, not treatment. The army offered the defense that psychoanalysis was unproven, impossible to administer considering the paucity of psychiatrists and the large number of mentally ill patients. The court supported the army illustrating the exceptional conditions of warfare (Eissler, 1986).

In the social upheavals following the Second World War, social philosophers argued that physicians were acting on behalf of the state when they hospitalized individuals. Objections to involuntary treatment became prominent in the United States during the Vietnam War and some state legislatures specifically prohibited the treatment of patients with ECT. In response, the American Psychiatric Association established a principle of voluntary consent to treatment with ECT (APA, 1978). It was an acknowledgement that the treatment was effective and that informed individual consent was essential to its proper use.

Informed Consent

Three concerns are reflected: the right of patients to receive ECT, the right to refuse treatment, and the nature of the information about the treatment and its hazards that is to be provided to assure informed consent. ECT is primarily used in severely ill patients who may not be fully able to comprehend the benefits and risks of the treatment, nor of the failure to accept the treatment. Such incompetent patients, admitted to hospitals under rules for involuntary admission, also have a right to be given ECT if it is the most appropriate way to assure remission of their illness and their release to the community. Indeed, involuntary patients who are not offered ECT when they are suffering from the conditions known to be responsive to ECT may contend that the treating physicians were negligent in omitting a medically indicated and highly effective treatment (Beresford, 1971).

Different conditions apply to competent persons who do not consent. Although it may be painful to watch a patient suffer or become more symptomatic, psychiatrists cannot invoke paternalism (*parens patriae*) to insist on a treatment that the patient refuses. The dilemma of informed consent, however, arises in the question of how much information is to be given to the patient (and his family) to ensure that consent is informed without frightening the patient so severely that he cannot consent when indicated.

Culver, Ferrell, and Green (1980) were among the first to analyze the meaning and the limitations of informed consent procedures. They argued that a depressive mood disorder, even one with suicidal features, does not necessarily render patients incapable of making informed decisions about their care. Typically, patients have had several previous episodes which have not responded to antidepressant drugs but respond excellently to ECT. They understand their situation and clearly prefer ECT to the options of the combination of psychotherapy and antidepressant medications with the likelihood of prolonged illness and unpleasant side effects. Both patients and psychiatrists recognize this situation. The authors give the following example.

INFORMED CONSENT—THE TYPICAL SITUATION

A 71-year-old-woman was admitted to hospital with a moderately severe depression. In the prior 40 years, she had suffered three depressive episodes. The third episode, six years earlier, was the most severe. She was treated with antidepressant medication. When this proved ineffective, ECT was recommended. She consented and received an effective course of treatment and her depression was relieved. She returned to an active life and was symptom-free for six years. Then, without a clear precipitant, she again became depressed with severe sleep disturbance, loss of appetite and weight, and thoughts of suicide. She was hospitalized and given antidepressant medication, which, as before, proved ineffective. She readily agreed to a course of ECT. Despite her illness, she was deemed capable of understanding her situation and making an informed decision about her treatment. She understood that ECT would almost certainly alleviate her depression as it had before, and she clearly preferred ECT to the options of no further treatment or combinations of antidepressant medications and psychotherapeutic support. After four treatments, her mood improved, her appetite and sleep pattern returned to normal, and her suicidal thoughts ceased. She was discharged and six months later remained in normal mood.

(Culver, Ferrell & Green, 1980)

Some patients, however, are not capable of consenting or not consenting. They are so ambivalent, a principal sign of their illness, that they cannot make a reasoned decision. Others withhold consent despite the advice of their physicians and relatives. Even when severely depressed and at risk of dying without treatment, patients may refuse ECT. Such situations may end tragically and are not limited to concerns about ECT. Frequently, patients in hospital who are offered a surgical procedure, a blood transfusion, or psychoactive medication refuse this care. Consultation-liaison psychiatrists are called to determine if the refusal of consent is rational or an irrational decision occasioned by incompetence related to dementia or psychosis. The implicit plea is that if the patient is seen as not competent, to declare the incompetence and thereby to allow the treatment as a life-saving measure. In such instances, psychiatrists differ in their responses, from initiation of treatment against the patients' wishes to respecting those wishes.

Culver and coworkers object to a practice where nonconsenting patients are regarded as incompetent and given treatment, although there is no independent measure of incompetence. The main danger of such quick and global labeling is that it may reassure the psychiatrist that a paternalistic insistence on treatment is justified, when it may not be. It is easier for psychiatrists to think they are treating noncompetent patients than to think they are forcing their own treatment decision on competent patients who disagree with it.

Criteria of Competence

Culver and coworkers offer the advice that a patient is competent to decide on a particular treatment when the patient understands that:

1. The physician believes the patient is ill and in need of treatment;
2. The physician believes a particular treatment may help the patient's illness; and,
3. The patient is being called upon to make the treatment decision.

The decisions made by a patient deemed competent according to these minimal criteria may either be rational or irrational, and in either instance, the treating team needs to follow the patient's wishes. Incompetent patients, however, are considered unable to make valid decisions, and the procedures assigned by law must be followed.

Confused patients, disoriented for time and place, unable to apprehend their surroundings, and exhibiting incoherent thinking and agitated behavior are considered incompetent to make treatment decisions. They give the following example.

INCOMPETENCE SECONDARY TO CONFUSION

A 69-year-old woman with a biopsy-proven non-operable retroperitoneal sarcoma was admitted in a profound delirium, resulting from systemic factors, psychotic depression, or a combination of the two. Approximately one year earlier, she had been admitted to the hospital in a similar mental state. At that time, a retroperitoneal mass had been identified and a biopsy obtained during the laparotomy. ECT had resulted in dramatic clearing of her confusional state, enabling her to reassume a satisfying life with her family. After 10 months, the confusional state recurred.

On admission, she was disoriented to place and time, severely agitated and restless. She was unable to give comprehensible answers to direct questions, and her speech consisted of incoherent babbling. An extensive search for a metabolic, pharmacological, or structural cause for her mental syndrome yielded no positive results. The sarcoma appeared to have increased in size, but this change could not be correlated with the change in mental function. The tumor was not considered life-threatening. Her physicians recommended ECT again but decided that she was not competent to give informed consent to any treatment procedure. The hospital attorney was of the opinion that ECT could be used if her three adult children could agree that treatment was indicated. The children consented, a course of ECT was administered, with a similar gratifying improvement.

(Culver, Ferrell & Green, 1980)

Irrational Refusal

More difficult situations are those in which patients deemed mentally competent make irrational decisions. They may refuse ECT because they believe that they are not that ill and do not warrant such treatment. Others may be terrified by the treatment, or cannot verbalize any reason at all. The following vignette, again from Culver and coworkers, illustrates this situation.

IRRATIONAL REFUSAL RESPECTED

A frail 55-year-old married woman was admitted with a six-month history of severe depression. Before admission her psychiatrist had prescribed two different antidepressant medications but had discontinued both because of severe hypotensive responses even to low starting doses. At intake, she was markedly depressed. She had lost a moderate amount of weight and was sleeping poorly but maintained an adequate intake of food and water. ECT was recommended but she firmly and consistently refused. She justified her decision by recalling that a close friend had received ECT for depression, and while the illness improved, she did kill herself a year later. The patient acknowledged that ECT may not have been responsible for the suicide but said she was terrified of the treatment. In that situation, she was again given an antidepressant. With careful nursing care, her orthostatic reaction proved manageable and after three weeks, her depression responded. Two weeks later, she was again feeling quite well, and hypotension was no longer a clinical problem.

(Culver, Ferrell & Green, 1980)

Despite the irrationality of her fears and beliefs, Culver and coworkers do not justify coercive efforts. The harm the patient risked by not choosing ECT was not deemed to be so great as to warrant overriding her autonomy. The decision of the patient was respected and alternative treatment offered.

Life at Stake

Only in the rare instance when ECT is necessary to save the life of a competent patient would paternalistic interventions be ethically defensible. Culver and coworkers give the following example.

LIFE AT RISK: SUBSTITUTED MEDICAL JUDGMENT

A 69-year-old married woman was admitted with a depressive illness of six months' duration. Approximately one year before admission she was discovered to have an enlarged spleen. No further studies were carried out. Approximately six months before her hospitalization, her husband suffered a heart attack and was subsequently confined to a nursing home. Her world "went into pieces." She became depressed and experienced changes in appetite, weight, and sleep. She refused medical attention. Eventually, her relatives called a lawyer, who summoned the police to her home, found her in a state of neglect, and brought her to the emergency room at her local hospital. She was admitted and noted to be depressed although she was alert, oriented, and cooperative. Positive physical findings included anemia, leucopenia, hypoproteinemia, and further increase in spleen size. A consulting psychiatrist recommended treatment with antidepressants. She agreed to take the medicine but did not improve. Her clinical condition continued to deteriorate and she refused food and fluids. She did not consent to bone marrow examination and other examinations, saying that she "didn't want to bother" and "I deserve to die." Her husband and son were informed of the risk of death through malnutrition and electrolyte disturbances. They applied to court and obtained temporary legal guardianship of the patient. The hematologist concluded that the most likely diagnosis was myelofibrosis. The long-term prognosis was poor but the prognosis for the next several years was quite good. The relatives authorized the psychiatrist to proceed with ECT.

Initially, she was treated without her consent and over stated objections. After the second treatment, however, she gave verbal consent to further treatments. After the fourth treatment, she was brighter in mood, ate well, and was verbal. After ten treatments, she felt quite well. A post-ECT delirium subsequently cleared. She expressed appropriate feelings of sadness about her husband's illness. She was grateful for having been treated. At a follow-up several months after discharge, she was well.

(Culver, Ferrell & Green, 1980)

According to the criteria, the patient was deemed competent. She refused ECT, however, giving no reason other than her belief that she deserved to die. This nontreatment choice was irrational and considered a reflection of a profound depressive illness. According to Culver and coworkers, a paternalistic intervention can be advocated when the harm or evil one is perpetrating has less weight than the evil one is forestalling. In ethical terms, the potential to "do good" outweighs the potential to "do harm"—beneficence outweighs nonmaleficence.

Conflicting Opinions

Culver and coworkers have not gone unchallenged. In a symposium reported in the *Journal of Medical Ethics* the American bioethicist Sherlock (1983) considered dubious the policy to respect irrational decisions by mentally competent patients. It implies that irrational decisions are permitted to override all other clinical and moral considerations. Sherlock maintains that severely depressed persons are not in a position to be autonomous. To foster the autonomy of the patient, the impediment represented by a severe psychiatric illness, such as a major depression, needs to be overcome. Sherlock also criticizes Culver and coworkers for not paying attention to the voluntary component of consent. A severely depressed individual is not free to consent, as a continuing irrational aversion to ECT, pathological indecisiveness, or phobic fears remove the capacity for an uncoerced choice. Such patients are best considered incompetent to render a voluntary consent. Sherlock argues that actions by caretakers in the name of paternalism are ethically defensible for patients who choose prolonged suffering over effective relief. Clinicians have a responsibility to act for the welfare of their patients.

The English philosopher Lesser (1983) agrees that competent but irrational decisions to refuse beneficial treatment should be overruled. To be relevant in the decision of competence, additional criteria are needed. For example, a patient may not be thinking clearly or may be unable to give understandable reasons for the decision. In practice, however, it may be difficult to be sure that the decision is irrational. The presumption is best made against coercion and the patient considered rational until proven to be irrational. Lesser points to the possibilities of offering alternative treatments acceptable to the patient or of persuading rather than forcing the patient to be treated. In practice, the position of Lesser is close to that of Culver and coworkers.

Taylor (1983), an English forensic psychiatrist, suggests that the optimal standard for making an informed decision is the affirmative answer of the psychiatrist to the patient's question: "If you were in my position, would you have this treatment?" She underscores the clinical importance of insuring that patients are given adequate information. She considers that patients occasionally may give irrational consent, for instance when psychotic depressed patients view ECT as deserved punishment. Such consent makes clinical management easier, but may be ethically dubious. Taylor also asks if refusal of ECT in the presence of severe depression can ever be deemed a competent decision.

An editorial (1983) in the same issue of the *Journal of Medical Ethics* discusses the conflict that arises between two principles of ethics, of doing good and respecting autonomy. The editorial pleads for enlarging the minimalist criteria of Culver and his colleagues in two respects. First, if a patient's perception of reality is distorted by delusions, illusions, or hallucinations, competence to reject treatment may be questioned even if minimalist criteria are fulfilled. Psychotic patients may not be competent to decide on treatment. Second, the criterion of voluntariness should be added—a requirement that the patient is in a state of mind in which he can make a voluntary decision. Again, the clearest examples of the opposite are in patients with psychotic disorders. The mere presence of a psychotic or other disorder, however, cannot in itself justify the assessment of incompetence to decide on treatment. Every patient must be judged for his specific personal condition.

Testing for Capacity to Consent

Martin and Bean (1992) maintain that a valid consent is a precondition to the administration of ECT and to be valid, the procedure must assess the capacity of the patient to consent. Although competence is an elusive concept, they argue for standardized test procedures that may justify the assessment and support the consent process. They offer specific questions to assess capacity. Instead of conceding the issue to government and to the legal profession to provide unclear statutory definitions, clinical assessments of competence may bring the issue of consent back to the domain of psychiatry.

Reiter-Theil (1992) maintains that the ethical message of informed consent does not require formalized testing and the signing of a legal contract. Rather, it means looking at the practice from the perspective of the patient. Testing of competence may lead to additional stress for the patient in the pretreatment period. Ignoring paternalistic behavior would not contribute to more respect for autonomy but imply neglect of the patients' interests for responsible treatment and care.

To assess legal competence to consent to treatment or research, the MacArthur Competence Assessment Tool for Treatment has been developed (Grisso & Appelbaum, 1998). It covers four abilities: understanding relevant information about disorder and treatment, reasoning about the potential risks and benefits of the choices, appreciation of the nature of the situation and the consequences of alternative choices, and ability to express a choice. The instrument has demonstrated good inter-rater reliability and validity as a capacity assessment tool.

The instrument was applied in a population of patients referred for ECT (Lapid et al., 2003). Most of the severely depressed patients who had been recommended for ECT appeared to have decisional capacity to give informed consent to the treatment. Education, including a discussion of the reasons for recommending ECT, followed by viewing of an ECT videotape with subsequent discussion of benefits, risks, and alternative treatments improved all four abilities. Psychotic patients had lower initial and final scores on appreciation as well as lower final scores on reasoning than nonpsychotic patients, but it was not clear whether nonpsychotic patients benefited more from education than psychotic patients. Half the patients received an additional discussion with a psychiatrist about ECT. It did not add measurably the decision making capacity.

Judicial Regulation

State laws in the United States regarding informed consent in ECT vary widely. Johnson (1993) discussed the effects of state regulations on physicians' abilities to provide comprehensive care to incompetent patients who are unable to give proper consent to treatment. Legislative and judicial efforts to regulate ECT that are aimed at protecting patients' rights result from public disapproval of ECT, combined with legitimate concerns regarding the condition of psychiatric facilities and the quality of care. Overcrowded and understaffed facilities, inadequate funding, poor living conditions, overuse of psychotropic drugs, and abuse of seclusion orders to discipline patients have concerned the public and the courts throughout the 20th century. A balance has to be established between the patient's liberty interests, the state's *parens patriae* power to act on behalf of the patient, and the state's duty to provide treatment.

The procedures to determine a patient's competence to make an informed decision polarized medical and legal communities. Most states require legal proceedings to appoint a guardian to represent the patient's interest, a judicial determination as to what the patient's interests may be, or both. Forty-three states in the United States regulate the use of ECT. Twenty states require a court determination of incompetence before treatment can be administered without the patient's consent. While these procedures are intended to defend the patient's interests, the extensive and detailed regulations impede the administration of treatment. It may take several weeks to schedule a court hearing, and even then approval is infrequently given. The courts have been reluctant to declare patients incompetent, making it even more difficult for truly incompetent individuals to receive treatment.

An example of California bureaucratic delay is found in the case of a young man described by his father Peter Wyden.

BUREAUCRATIC DELAY IN CONSENT

Jeff had a chronic psychotic illness with multiple hospitalizations and prolonged treatments. During one hospital period in California, his illness became so severe that ECT was recommended. Physical restraints and isolation were required. In preparation for ECT, his physicians suspended all medication. Court approval was requested but the go-ahead from the judge was long in coming. That was especially outrageous since four local psychiatrists had recommended the treatment urgently as well as three teams of consultants. Phone appeals to various officials yielded nothing and only a telegram from the parents to the judge could make ECT start. Jeff returned

to his healthy, witty, and self-assured self, although a relapse occurred after
three months.

(Wyden, 1998)

Another example of the impact of legal impediments in patient care is a
young woman with manic-depressive illness who had been unresponsive to
many medications in a stormy clinical course for more than a year. A decision was made to treat her with ECT, but as she was grossly psychotic and
considered incapable of consenting, approval from a California court was
requested.

LEGAL IMPEDIMENTS TO TREATMENT (1)

There were overwhelming legal and bureaucratic difficulties in obtaining court
approval. The legal difficulties consisted primarily of a precedent not to give
court approval for ECT to patients who are unable to give informed consent;
the bureaucratic difficulties entailed the confusion, disagreement, and uncer-
tainty of all administrative levels over the proper procedure for obtaining such
requests. It became clear that it was not going to be feasible to treat Ms. A
with ECT.

[Because the patient could not be cared for at the acute psychiatric inpatient ward, she was transferred to a state facility, where she died. The author
concludes her letter with the comment:]

I write in hope of assisting a necessary change in public attitudes toward
real priorities, which are to provide better treatment as well as to ensure individual rights. They should not have to be mutually exclusive.

(Parry, 1981)

In the State of Alabama, the laws are particularly strict for patients unable
to voluntarily consent. The patient or a family member must ask for court
review of the decision to use ECT before the treatment begins. Where the
emergency use of ECT is required, the procedures to obtain approval of
treatment are even more rigorous. While designed to protect both the competent and incompetent from hasty decisions without full consideration of a
patient's best interest, such regulations create severe, often insurmountable,
hurdles to effective treatment and care. A particularly egregious example is
reported from the University of Michigan.

LEGAL IMPEDIMENTS TO TREATMENT (2)

Ms. J, a 21-year-old intelligent and active young woman with no prior psychiatric history, developed a malar rash, diffuse arthralgias, and occasional
episodes of chest pain and shortness of breath. With confirming laboratory
studies, the diagnosis of systemic lupus erythematosus (SLE) was made. With-

in a month of conventional medical therapies, she experienced intermittent bizarre behaviors and described auditory hallucinations, accompanied by worsening systemic symptoms. When the psychotic symptoms became persistent, she was admitted to hospital for treatment with antipsychotic agents. An MRI scan of the head was consistent with lupus cerebritis and high-dose steroids was prescribed. Her mental status worsened with superimposed catatonic symptoms of posturing, stereotypic movements, echolalia, and echopraxia.

She was transferred to the University of Michigan Hospital in Ann Arbor where the diagnosis of SLE was confirmed and medical treatment continued. Because of the severity of her systemic illnes, predominance of catatonia, and failure to respond to antipsychotic medications, ECT was recommended.

Ms. J was mute and not able to consent to ECT. Her mother and grandmother, who were very active in the patient's ongoing care, were in agreement with ECT but did not hold guardianship or durable power of attorney to consent on the patient's behalf. In consultation with the hospital attorney, the judgment was made that since the patient was hospitalized on a medical service with catatonia secondary to her medical condition, ECT was assessed as an emergency medical, rather than psychiatric intervention, that could be administered without explicit guardianship or commitment. Her next of kin (her mother) served as the consentor.

The patient received six ECT and resumed spontaneous speech, diminished psychosis, and lessened catatonia. Her medical care no longer justified treatment on an in-patient medical service and transfer to the psychiatry service was considered. But a transfer to the psychiatry service would place her care under the jurisdiction of the Michigan Mental Health Code which states that to initiate "a procedure intended to produce convulsions or coma" there must be either consent from the patient (if older than 18), consent from a parent (if a minor), consent from a guardian or durable power of attorney, or consent from the probate court "if an individual eligible to give consent for the procedure is not located after a diligent effort." The code also states that authority for a guardian or a durable power of attorney to consent to ECT must be explicitly stated in the guardianship or durable power of attorney (DPOA) papers (Michigan Act 258 of 1974, 330.1717 sec 717).

Although she was not well, the patient was discharged with the recommendation to continue outpatient ECT. On the way to her first outpatient appointment, she became severely agitated and violent, and sought to jump out of the moving vehicle. Upon arrival at the hospital she was taken directly to the psychiatric emergency room. She was mute, negativistic, echopractic with prominent stereotyped movements. She would not participate in a voluntary admission, and was admitted to the inpatient psychiatry unit on petition and certification.

The laboratory tests for SLE had improved but her mental state had wors-

ened. She reported auditory and visual hallucinations. She had multiple catatonic signs and exhibited episodes in which she would lie rigidly on the floor
with fluttering eyes. The possibility of seizures was considered and lorazapam
administered. She was maintained on one-to-one supervision for periodic agitation and aggression.

Now under the jurisdiction of the Michigan Mental Health Code, ECT could
no longer be considered an emergency medical intervention. She could no
longer be given ECT until either permission from a guardian or probate court
certification could be obtained. The patient's mother filed the papers for
guardianship, but the hearing could not be scheduled for many weeks. After
12 days, court-ordered treatments, including ECT, were obtained. She
received her first ECT the morning of the hearing.

After ECT was resumed, Ms. J became more responsive and interactive,
denied auditory or visual hallucinations, and exhibited decreased stereotypic
movements. Her systemic illness worsened, interfering with the course of ECT.
Obtaining IV access became difficult and a central intravenous port was surgi-
cally installed. During this disruption, she again acted bizarrely, frequently
agitated and angry, with a recurrence of auditory and visual hallucinations.

When ECT was resumed, Ms. J again demonstrated rapid improvement in
symptoms and after a sustained course over two weeks, both the patient and
her family felt that she had returned to 80–90% of her baseline. She was
much more interactive and vocal, denied hallucinations, and demonstrated
neither muscle rigidity nor motor stereotypies. She was discharged from the
hospital and after six months has not shown the recurrence of catatonic or psychotic symptoms.

(Maixner & Krain, personal communication)

The patient experienced delays and interferences in the administration of
ECT occasioned by legal requirements that placed ECT in a special catego-
ry of treatments. She suffered from a systemic illness with psychiatric
manifestations that are responsive to ECT (Guze, 1967; Kronfol et al., 1977;
Mac & Pardo, 1983; Fricchione et al., 1990). It was acceptable to offer the
patient medical treatments and even administer antipsychotic medications
without her specific consent, but ECT, the specific and necessary psychiatric
treatment, could not be administered. The stricter legal standard to which
ECT is held did the patient no service; indeed, it prolonged her illness and
materially increased the number of treatments that she required.

In New York State, a court determination of incompetence is not required
before administering ECT. It may be given to a patient who lacks the capacity to consent following a medical determination of the decisional capacity
and the substituted consent of a person—usually a family member—

authorized to act on the patient's behalf. The chief of service of the treatment facility and an independent qualified consultant not employed by the facility are charged with making the decision of competence and the need for treatment. Oregon follows a similar procedure.

While it has often been argued that determinations of competence should be left to the courts, Endler and Persad (1988) maintain that quasi-judicial hearings and court proceedings remove the advantage of the intimate knowledge and caring attitude that usually characterizes the relationship of patients with their doctors.

In Europe, compulsory admissions vary twenty-fold among different countries (Zinkler & Priebe, 2002). The criteria for compulsory admission of the mentally ill are broadly similar when it comes to patients at risk to themselves or others, but differ for involuntary treatment in the interest of the patients' health. The variation is influenced by professional ethics and attitudes, sociodemographic variables, public preoccupation about risk arising from mental illness, and legal frameworks. Appropriate international comparisons are difficult due to the absence of comparable definitions and problems of translation.

Swedish constitutional law respects the equal worth of all its citizens and the freedom and dignity of the individual. The aim of compulsory psychiatric care is to enable patients to take part in continued voluntary care. Compulsory care is only allowed in severe psychotic disorders and depression with the risk of suicide. Dangerousness for others is also a consideration. Courts are not involved but admission is based on the judgment of two doctors, one who refers and the other, a specialist in psychiatry, who admits the patient. If care needs to be extended beyond four weeks, a court must be consulted for further incarceration. With court permission, care may be given for another four months and thereafter, for six months at a time. A compulsory-admitted patient has the right to have a supporting person to assist in court contacts and personal matters. If possible, the treatment during compulsory care should be in consultation with the patient, but treatment may be given without the patient's consent. Nearest relatives are informed but treatment decisions remain with the psychiatrist. At court it is only possible to appeal against restraints of freedom, not treatment decisions.

Hidden coercion, defined as coercion without support in the law, has rarely been addressed. In some venues, the limit between voluntary and involuntary care is not as strict as desirable (Eriksson & Westrin, 1995). Voluntarily admitted patients often experience coercion, for instance, when given injections of neuroleptic drugs or prohibited to leave the department. The border between persuasion and coercion is unclear.

Paternalistic Intervention

The jurist MacDonald (1984) pays special attention to paternalistic intervention in relation to hospital admission status. Accepting the proposition that individual liberty must be secondary to fostered autonomy and assuming that an involuntary patient has been institutionalized on the basis of dangerous behavior, he finds it reasonable that those who are in dire need of ECT but refuse to accept it should nevertheless undergo the treatment. In fact, patients could not be involuntarily detained unless appropriate medical treatment is offered. As for nonconsenting voluntary patients, the administration of ECT may encompass an intrusive violation of the patient whose wishes should be respected. As acknowledged by legal authorities, however, the border between voluntary and involuntary consent is imprecise. If voluntary patients are unable to care for themselves outside the hospital, discharging them would show a cruel disrespect for their welfare. Leaving them in their present condition of illness and hospitalization would be equally cruel. Under such circumstances, MacDonald considers it best to inform patients of their inevitable committal as involuntary patients and that clinically indicated treatment as ECT may be given. MacDonald is skeptical of surrogate consent since it raises as many ethical issues as it purports to resolve. Ultimately, to deny a clinically useful therapy may be worse than applying a speculatively detrimental one.

In a survey of psychiatric ethics, the Canadian psychiatrist Merskey (1999) defends a paternalistic position on ECT in some psychotic patients.

The Rule of Double Effect

In the Middle Ages, Roman Catholic moral theologians developed the rule of double effect to be applied to situations in which it is impossible to avoid all harmful actions (Quill et al., 1997). Under this rule, an action having good as well as harmful actions is permissible if:

1. The act itself is good or at least morally neutral;
2. Only the good effect is intended;
3. The good effect is not achieved through the bad effect;
4. There is no alternative way to obtain the good effect; and
5. There is a proportionally grave reason for running the risk.

Medical ethicists cite the rule of double effect to explain why clinicians are permitted to administer high doses of opioid analgesics to relieve pain in terminally ill patients, even in amounts that could cause the patient to die sooner than otherwise (Pellegrino, 1998).

Apart from end-of-life decision making, the rule has been used to justify more densely spaced ECT than the regular intervals of two or three days (Little, personal communication). The conditions are fulfilled since such treatment relieves suffering; only the relief of suffering and not the increased cognitive effects is intended; the alleviation does not depend on cognitive impairment; medication or conventional ECT has not been successful; and the relief of intolerable suffering is a proportionally grave reason for running the risk. The rule of double effect gives the psychiatrist an ethical base from which a flexible administration of ECT may be considered in exceptional clinical circumstances. With the same justification ECT may also be used to treat psychiatric illness comorbid with mental retardation.

Summary

Informed voluntary consent is a paramount consideration in the practice of medicine. It is particularly relevant in psychiatric practice where psychiatric illnesses may interfere with the ability of patients to understand the offered information and the ability to consent to treatments. Under such circumstances, psychiatrists and ethicists have formulated rules for when autonomy must be respected and when treatment has the overriding priority. While all authors agree that incompetent patients cannot make valid decisions, opinions differ as how to judge individual competency and whether competent patients who make irrational decisions should be treated against their wishes. Unanimity exists, however, that patients should be treated against their wishes when failure to do so risks loss of life. Coercion can usually be avoided but it is inhumane not to use it if persuasion is not successful. A paternalistic position on ECT for some psychotic patients may be defended. Judicial regulation may be an impediment to a rational medical handling and may counteract the aim to protect patients' civil rights.

CHAPTER 4

Beneficence

Those who are ill look to physicians for relief and treatments are offered if their benefits are well defined and are achievable at tolerable risk. Many interventions are usually available for each illness, competing in the marketplace in efficacy, cost, speed of onset, and toxicity. In assessing interventions, the good that they do is their principal justification. In this review, we discuss the usefulness of ECT in clinical practice today.

Convulsive therapy was originally introduced for patients with schizophrenia. The ease of its use led to experiments in other psychiatric illnesses and it was soon found to be effective in a range of psychiatric disorders including depression, especially the psychotic type, in mania and delirious mania, in postpartum psychosis, and in schizoaffective disorders (APA, 2001; Abrams, 2002a). ECT proved particularly effective in malignant catatonia and neuroleptic malignant syndrome, illnesses that are associated with high fatality rates (Fink & Taylor, 2003). It may also relieve rigidity in patients with Parkinson syndrome (Andersen et al., 1987; Douyon et al., 1989; Rasmussen & Abrams, 1991) and be life-saving in acute deliria (Fink, 1999b). It may provide relief when medications fail. These attributes are the principal basis for its continued use.

The illnesses in which ECT is effective have high levels of disability, mortality, and morbidity and contribute strongly to the global burden of disease (Murray & Lopez, 1996, 1997a, b). Indeed, estimates of the ten leading causes of disability worldwide finds unipolar major depression as the second highest, sandwiched between ischaemic heart disease and road traffic accidents (Murray & Lopez, 1997b). It is in major depression that the evidence for the efficacy of ECT is most compelling (UK ECT Group, 2003).

The National Institute of Mental Health (NIMH) has announced that a major health goal is to reduce years of life lived with disabilities (YLDs) associated with major depression by 10% by the year 2010 (National Advisory

Mental Health Council 2003). Another estimate by the WHO finds unipolar depression as 4.4% of total global burden of disease calculated from disability adjusted years (Reynolds, 2003).

Depressive Mood Disorders

The evidence for the antidepressant efficacy of ECT is extensive, beginning with the reports that the duration of illness and death rates for patients with manic-depressive insanity and involutional depression were reduced (Ziskind et al., 1945; Huston & Locher, 1948; Fishbein, 1949; Bond, 1954a, b). In a study of 300 depressed inpatients, ECT was compared with the tricyclic antidepressant imipramine, the monoamine oxidase (MAO) inhibitors phenelzine and isocarboxazid, and placebo (Greenblatt et al., 1964). After eight weeks, the percentage of patients practically symptom-free and capable of functioning in society was 76% in the ECT group, and 46% to 50% for imipramine, MAO inhibitors, and placebo. ECT was superior in all depressive subtypes except among those identified as suffering from "neurotic depression" who improved irrespective of treatment.

A similar design was used in a British study (Medical Research Council, 1965) in which the condition for inclusion was a persistent alteration of mood exceeding customary sadness, accompanied by self-depreciation, retardation, agitation, sleep disturbance, or hypochondria. Depression was primary, that is, not arising from other mental disorder. Hospitalized patients were randomly allocated to ECT, imipramine, phenelzine, or placebo. After four weeks, the rates of marked improvement were 71% for ECT, 52% for imipramine, 30% for phenelzine, and 39% for placebo. When dividing the patients in groups of severe (with delusions or suicidal ideas) and moderate depression, ECT was the only treatment superior to placebo among those with severe depression (66% versus 42%). Among moderately ill, ECT still being superior (77% improved), imipramine was more effective than placebo (59% versus 37%). Several other studies showed the superiority of ECT over all other treatments in severe depressive illness (Hordern et al., 1965; Carney et al., 1965; Mendels, 1965; Glassman et al., 1975). A meta-analysis of ten comparative trials up to 1985 confirmed this superiority over tricyclic antidepressant drugs and MAO inhibitors (Imlah et al., 1965).

The most recent meta-analysis finds real ECT to be significantly more effective than simulated ECT and more effective than pharmacotherapy in depressive disorders. The authors conclude: "There is a reasonable evidence base for the use of ECT; it does not rest simply on anecdote, habit, and tradition.... ECT remains an important treatment option for the management of severe depression." (ECT Review Group, 2003, p. 807). A similar conclusion is presented by a second independent meta-analysis of ECT in depression (Kho et al., 2003).

ECT implies more extensive preparation of patients and may have a stronger psychological impact than antidepressant drugs. Trials have been made to control such influence. A study from India showed that ECT combined with placebo was superior to imipramine-augmented sham ECT, an identical procedure with real ECT except no induction of convulsive activity (Gangadhar et al., 1982). With the same purpose, six concurrent studies in various departments of psychiatry in the United Kingdom compared the efficacy of real ECT to sham ECT. Real ECT was superior to sham ECT in five (Freeman et al., 1978; West, 1981; Johnstone et al., 1980; Brandon et al., 1984; Gregory et al., 1985); the sixth used too low energies in the less effective form of unilateral ECT (Lambourn & Gill, 1978). The weighted rates of improvement in the five adequate studies were 68% versus 37%.

Despite the evidence of these many studies, professional and public antipathy has so stigmatized ECT that even knowledgeable upper social class patients, hospitalized at prestigious academic hospitals, have no guarantee of getting the treatment. Yale Professor of Surgery Sherwin Nuland writes about his illness, which occurred in the early 1970s.

PERSONAL EXPERIENCE WITH ECT (1)

From my late thirties until my early forties, I underwent a period of depression that gradually deepened into an intensity that I finally required admission to a mental hospital, where I stayed for more than a year. Neither medication, psychotherapy, the determined efforts of friends nor the devotion of the few people whose love never deserted me had even the most minimal beneficial effect on my worsening state of mind. Finally, faced with my resistance to all forms of treatment till then attempted, the senior psychiatrists at the institution in which I was confined recommended the draconian measure of lobotomy.

I was, in fact, completely disabled by pathological preoccupations and fears. Obsessions with coincidences; fixations on recurrent numbers; feelings of worthlessness and physical or sexual inadequacy; religious anxieties of guilt and concerns about God's will; ritualistic thinking and behavior—they crowded in on one another so forcefully as to occupy every lacuna of my mind. I cowered before them, not only emotionally but physically, too—my hunched-over posture reflected my decline into helplessness.

I was saved from the drastic intervention of lobotomy by the refusal of a twenty-seven-year-old resident psychiatrist assigned to my case to agree with his teachers. At his insistence, a course of electroshock therapy was reluctantly embarked upon. I would learn later that virtually everyone familiar with my case despaired of the possibility of recovery.

At first, the newly instituted treatment made not a whit of difference. The number of electroshock treatments mounted, but still no improvement took place. The total would eventually reach twenty. Somewhere around the middle of the course, a glimmer of change made itself evident, which encouraged the skeptical staff to continue a series of treatments they had begun only to mollify a promising young man in training. I recovered so well, in fact, that in the four remaining months of hospitalization, I lost all but the dimmest memory of the obsessions and saw my depression disappear entirely.

For seventeen years, I was free of any hint of depression. But in the past decade, I have had a few recurrences, though none remotely approaching the catastrophe of thirty years ago, and none accompanied by more than a whiff of obsessional thinking. When the old pain begins to make its presence known, I return to the wisdom—and the presence—of the former psychiatric resident who saved my life and my sanity.

(Nuland, 2003)

The professor returned to surgery, teaching, and writing, and in the decades since has written widely acclaimed books. His symptoms were evidence of an agitated psychotic depression with obsessional features, a condition that is eminently responsive to ECT. The obsessions, in all probability, led to the consideration of psychosurgery. A tragedy was averted by the courage of a subordinate physician to stand up for his beliefs.

A similar near-tragedy was experienced by Dr. Osheroff, a dentist who was admitted to the Chestnut Lodge, a prestigious private sanitarium outside Washington, D.C. in the early 1990s. Prolonged psychoanalytic treatment did him no service and after he had become systemically ill, he was transferred to a general hospital and treated effectively (Klerman, 1990; Stone, 1990). In a malpractice suit against the hospital for failure to offer effective treatment, the hospital agreed to settlement (Packman et al., 1994).

Norman Endler, the Canadian Professor of Psychology, described his travail with depression, the failure to respond to medications that induced severe side effects, and his recovery with ECT. Afterward, he wrote about the treatment.

PERSONAL EXPERIENCE WITH ECT (2)

A needle was injected into my arm and I was told to count back from 100. I got about as far as 91. The next thing I knew I was in the recovery room.. I was slightly groggy and tired but not confused. My memory was not impaired. I certainly knew where I was. . . .

After about the third or fourth treatment, I began to feel somewhat better.

My last ECT session was the next morning [September 16-treatment #6], and that evening my wife and I went to a symphony concert.... On the next Wednesday, September 21, I taught my first class; I also played my first game of tennis in more than three months and won. That night my sex drive returned—my holiday of darkness was over....

[In a postscript, Dr. Endler writes] Negative attitudes about ECT die hard. A few months later ... I phoned a friend who is a professor of psychology and a clinician.... When we met I told him about my depression and about ECT. His response was "Oh, my gosh! How could you let them do this to you, Norm."

(Endler, 1982)

Martha Manning, an American psychologist and psychotherapist, described her experience with severe depression. Her professional training and experience brought her to the eventual realization that she fulfilled more of the criteria of major depression, as a matter of fact all of them, than did her patients. Psychotherapy and reassurance from colleagues were insufficient to assure relief and reluctantly she concluded that the depression was not psychologically determined but had a biological, probably hereditary, origin. Antidepressant and sedative drugs gave troublesome side effects and only temporary relief. Thoughts of death and suicide became more and more intrusive. She was hospitalized, given six ECT, and recovered. She poignantly describes the prejudice of her colleagues and friends against her decision for medication and ECT, and wonders why the attitude is so dissimilar to another electric treatment, that of electroconversion of a cardiac arrest, which is also lifesaving.

PERSONAL EXPERIENCE WITH ECT (3)

Telling people I've had ECT is a real conversation killer. People seem more forthright these days [1995] about discussing depression. Hell, the cashier in the grocery store told me yesterday that she's on Prozac. But ECT is in a different class. For months I have glossed over ECT's contribution to the end of my depression in my conversations with most people. But lately I've been thinking, "Damn it. I didn't rob a bank. I didn't kill anybody. I have nothing to be ashamed of." I've started telling people about ECT. My admission is typically met with uncomfortable silences and abrupt shifts in topics.

An acquaintance at a party is outraged. "How could you let them do that to you?" I bristle and answer, "I didn't let them do it to me. I asked them to do it."

(Manning, 1994)

Martha Manning returned to her clinical practice and the care of her family.

The latest witness to the tragedy of manic depressive illness is Leon Rosenberg, former dean of Yale Medical School and head of pharmaceutical research for Bristol-Myers-Squibb, and now professor of molecular biology at Princeton University. In 1998, around his 65th birthday, awakening in an agitated state after restless nights of insomnia, he attempted suicide by drug overdose. He was admitted to the closed ward of a psychiatric hospital. ECT was prescribed.

PERSONAL EXPERIENCE WITH ECT (4)

However groggy I still was, I registered surprise. I thought that ECT had been abandoned years before.

[Treatment began] After the fourth ECT, I was noticeably less depressed. My appetite returned, as did my ability to sleep. After eight treatments, my mood was fully restored. I experienced no confusion, memory loss, headache, or any other symptom sometimes attributed to ECT. I felt so well that, with some trepidation, I prepared to go back to work.

[Lithium continuation sustained the benefit. He decided to bear witness.]

I now understand that I was brainsick ("diseased of the brain and mind") when I tried to kill myself. I view my suicide attempt as the end result of mental illness in the same way I view a heart attack as the end result of coronary artery disease. Both are potentially lethal, both have known risk factors, both are major public health problems, both are treatable and preventable, and both generate fear and grief. But the shame associated with them differs greatly. Heart attack victims are consoled ("Isn't it a pity?"), suicide victims are cursed ("How could he?")

[Dr. Rosenberg's illness began at age 26 when, after finishing two years of residency training in medicine, he describes crying over nothing; his sense of self-worth had evaporated; and he lost pleasure in his family. The funk lasted several weeks. A second episode and others were precipitated when he made professional moves.]

Some of my depressive bouts would last a month; others hung on for two or three. I felt like everything—movement, thought, speech—took more energy. I had trouble connecting with either my family or my associates.

[On the other hand] I liked the way my mind worked during the long intervals when I wasn't depressed. I could work 16 to 18 hours daily, write papers quickly, make original scientific connections, speak articulately, and interact with associates and family pleasurably.

[In an aside, Dr. Rosenberg comments] Because ECT is offered at a relatively small number of hospitals, I find myself wondering what would have happened to me had I not been referred to one of them.

(Rosenberg, 2002)

As a manic-depressive academic in a leading position, Dr. Rosenberg decided that going public about his treatment could help destigmatize both mental illness and ECT.

Psychotic Depression

The more severe forms of depression described as "psychotic depression" have a more rapid and the more complete treatment response to ECT than do the milder, nonpsychotic forms of the illness. Psychotic depression was demarcated as a diagnostic subtype of psychiatric illness in 1975 (Glassman et al., 1975). In treating hospitalized depressed patients with imipramine at doses that were monitored by serum levels, the researchers found patients who failed the medication trial but subsequently recovered with ECT. It was the presence of delusions that marked the subgroup of nonresponders to imipramine.

This differential effect of treatment was confirmed in a large Italian study published in 1964, translated and republished in 1979 (deCarolis et al., 1964; Avery & Lubrano, 1979). Of nearly 300 patients with endogenous depression, 61% responded to imipramine (200–350 mg) within 30 days. The nonresponders were treated with 8 to 10 bilateral ECT and 85% then improved. In the subgroup of nearly 200 patients with psychotic depression (with depressive delusions) only 40% had responded to imipramine and of these, 83% subsequently were relieved with ECT. The superiority of ECT over antidepressant drugs has been repeatedly confirmed in evaluations of clinical reports (Kroessler, 1985; Parker et al., 1992; Wheeler Vega et al., 2000; Kho et al., 2003).

The superiority of ECT in psychotic depression was again demonstrated in the latest report from the NIMH-supported four-hospital collaborative study of major depression treated with bitemporal ECT (Petrides et al., 2001). Of 253 patients who completed an ECT course of three treatments weekly, 30% met criteria for psychotic depression. Of these, 95% remitted; of the nonpsychotic depressed patients, 84% remitted, for an overall remission rate of 87%. This experience has been confirmed by an independent study that reported a 92% response rate for patients with psychotic depression compared to 55% for those with nonpsychotic depression treated with ECT (Birkenhäger et al., 2003). Indeed, the efficacy of ECT is so high that ECT has been considered a primary treatment, especially in patients who are severely psychotic and suicidal (APA, 1993, 2001).

Yet, despite the compelling evidence of clinical research, the role of ECT in treating psychotic depression is marginalized in two ways. Expert treatment algorithms consider ECT as the third, fourth, or last resort after numerous medication trials (Crismon et al., 1999; American Psychiatric

Association, 2000). A more insidious denigration of the role of ECT is in the review papers on psychiatric treatments that frequently dot the literature. A chapter on "New Approaches to Managing Psychotic Depression" in a journal supplement dedicated to managing difficult-to-treat depressions is one example (Thase, 2003a). After emphasizing the roles of new antidepressants, atypical antipsychotic drugs, and combinations in the main body of the report, Schatzberg (2003), as an afterthought in a section on other treatments concludes: "While there are sufficient data to recommend ECT for the treatment of psychotic depression, there are both real and perceived drawbacks to ECT; therefore it may be best considered after other options have failed" (p. 21). Instead, a medication that is undergoing clinical trials and not approved for marketing for this disorder is discussed.

Cost-Effectiveness

In a comparison of treatment with ECT and antidepressant drugs, patients given ECT stayed an average of 13 fewer days, which means considerable saving of resources. In addition to the therapeutic advantages, economic benefits speak in favor of a more frequent use of ECT for severely depressed inpatients (Markowitz et al., 1987).

In a U.S. survey of general hospital inpatients in 1993, 9.4% of the patients with major depression received ECT (Olfson et al., 1998). While most patients with major depression received ECT after trials of other treatments, making their stays more costly, those patients treated within the first five days of admission found their stays to be shorter and less costly. Prompt administration of ECT was associated with shorter stays and lower costs. A case report and a letter describing a similar experience define substantial saving when outpatient ECT was prescribed instead of admitting the patient to hospital (Bonds et al., 1998; Steffens et al., 1995).

Suicide Risk

Suicide and suicide attempts are risks of the major psychiatric illnesses, with mortality rates markedly higher than for the general population (Harris & Barraclough, 1997). Recent estimates find the lifetime risk for those ever hospitalized to be about 9%, with a lifetime risk of up to 4% for all persons with depressive illness.

Sixty percent of suicides occur in the year after depression with the first three months as the most dangerous period (Bostwick & Pankratz, 2000). Incomplete resolution of depression is a principal factor in relapse of depression with medication treatment (Bostwick & Pankratz, 2000; Oquendo et al., 2002; Isometsa et al., 1996). At one year follow-up after medication treatment, 20% of the remitted patients and 80% of the improved patients had relapsed. (Thase, 1999, 2003b).

The risk of suicide is particularly severe in depressed patients ill enough to be hospitalized (Roose et al., 1983; Coryell & Winokur, 1992; Spiessel, 2002). Profound hopelessness, hypochondriacal ruminations or delusions, and thoughts of suicide or self-harm during depression predict suicide (Schneider et al., 2001). An ongoing study cited below reports a 3% incidence of suicide attempts among the patients referred for ECT, and active suicidal thoughts, threats, gestures in 27% (Kellner et al., submitted).

Medications are the principal agents used to treat these disorders today. Their impact on suicide risk is not well defined. Avery and Winokur (1978) examined the six months postdepression course of 519 patients, and found that 0.8% of ECT patients made a subsequent suicide attempt compared to 4.2% for those receiving adequate courses of antidepressant drugs, and 7% of patients receiving inadequate courses.

A review of the FDA files for antidepressant medications approved between 1985 and 2000 showed similar suicide rates in patients randomized to newly approved SSRI medications (0.59%), standard comparison antidepressants (0.76%), and placebo (0.45%) (Khan et al., 2000). The authors concluded that the medications were no more effective than placebo in reducing suicide rates.

In a review of the evidence for the impact of ECT on suicide rates, Tanney (1986) found the incidence of suicide during the ECT era (after 1938) to be less than before the introduction of ECT. Citing nine studies in addition to Avery and Winokur noted above, the rate of suicide decreased in seven studies and remained unchanged in two. Prudic and Sackeim (1999) reported a profound short-term effect of ECT on suicidal behavior, but little evidence for a long-term effect, in their review of the literature on ECT and suicide. Interestingly, they reported an overall reduction in mortality in ECT treated patients unrelated to the effect on suicide risk. In their treatment of depressed patients with right unilateral ECT, they recorded a marked reduction in the scores on the suicide item (Item 3) of the Hamilton Depression Scale. The impact of ECT on the suicide item was great, independent of whether the overall depression score was reduced or not.

In an ongoing multisite, NIMH-funded, collaborative ECT study in patients with major depression, 444 patients with unipolar major depression received bilateral ECT (Kellner et al., submitted). Assessing suicide risk with the Hamilton Depression Scale, 118 had active suicidal thoughts, actions, or gestures, and 13 reported a suicide event during the present illness. With ECT administered three times a week, the ratings of suicide risk successively dropped to zero for almost all patients: 27% after one ECT, 60% after 3 ECT (one week), 81% after 6 ECT (two weeks), and 90% after nine treatments (three weeks).

Considering the risk of suicide and the delayed efficacy of medications, the practice of recommending ECT as a last resort option in expert treatment algorithms puts the suicidal patient at unnecessary risk. The rapid relief with ECT warrants earlier consideration in treatment planning.

Postpartum Psychosis

Acute depressive psychoses are frequently reported immediately following delivery of an infant and occasionally late during a pregnancy. In Europe, such episodes are considered cycloid psychoses. ECT is rapidly and reliably effective, thereby allowing resumed breast-feeding and nursing care (Perris, 1974). The anesthetic medications used in ECT are not harmful to the infant, while some medications, such as lithium and the benzodiazepines, may accumulate in the breast milk and influence the infant's development. The desirability to avoid all drugs during lactation makes ECT preferable to pharmacologic therapy in these dramatic psychoses. The following case report is an example.

POSTPARTUM PSYCHOSIS

A 38-year-old woman had delivered her first child after a protracted but otherwise complication-free labor. The fine healthy boy, weighing 3400 g, was much longed for. The relationship with the husband was harmonious. After the delivery, she slept badly, felt increasing anxiety, and paced in her room repeatedly. She feared that somebody would to poison or otherwise hurt the child, saying that it is malformed and that her genitals were destroyed at the delivery. At first, the illness was episodic, but gradually the mental disorder became continuous.

After transfer to the Psychiatric Department, she was seen to weep and laugh by turns, and not to recognize the personnel.

The clinical picture was considered typical of a cycloid psychosis with a mixture of anxiety, confusion, delusions, and mood changes. After four ECT, given every second day, she regained her healthy self. She could nurse the baby at her breast and she was discharged from the hospital after two weeks' care.

(Ottosson, 2004)

---

to twenty treatments in a single course, others were examined periodically with interim ECT offered as soon as signs of relapse appeared. Such continuation treatment was successful (Karliner & Wehrheim, 1965). With the introduction of antidepressant drugs, many clinicians believed that the medicines would replace ECT, both as a primary treatment and as a continuation treatment. Experience found many patients, however, for whom the drugs were unsatisfactory as the primary treatment and ECT was called back into clinical use (Abrams, 1988, 2002; Fink, 1999). Continuation ECT has gradually been reintroduced into clinical practice and increasing numbers of patients are now being treated as outpatients in prolonged courses measured in months (Kramer, 1987, 1990; Fink et al., 1996; Fink, 1999; Gagne et al., 2000; Abrams, 2002a). For example, in a retrospective chart review Gagne and colleagues (2000) identified 29 patients who received continuation ECT plus antidepressant treatment after successful course of ECT for major depression and matched their course with an equal number of patients who received antidepressant drugs alone after ECT. The mean duration of follow-up was 3.9 years. In this nonrandomized comparison, outcome was better in the continuation ECT group. The cumulative probability of surviving without relapse or recurrence at 2 years was 93% for continuation ECT patients and 52% for antidepressant-alone patients. At 5 years, survival declined to 73% for continuation ECT patients, but fell to 18% for antidepressant-alone patients. Mean survival times were 6.9 years for the continuation ECT patients and 2.7 years for the antidepressant-alone patients.

A controlled study comparing the benefits of continuation ECT with combined lithium and nortriptyline is ongoing, with reports expected in 2004.

Since ECT patients are free from symptoms when they agree to continuation treatment, there can be no concern about their consent as voluntary and informed. When the treatment is given on an out-patient basis, the patients can walk or cycle to and from the treatment, or get to and from the hospital with the assistance of relatives or friends. Where continuation ECT is practiced, it has contributed to defusing concerns about the treatment.

Technical Aspects

In electrical inductions, seizure quality and antidepressant benefit vary with electrode placement (unilateral, bitemporal, or bifrontal) and by energy dosing (various multiples of calibrated seizure threshold, by age-derived formulae, or visual monitoring of the EEG).

Bilateral stimulation through electrodes on both temples was the original-nal mode of application. As the left hemisphere of the brain is the primary center of verbal memory, unilateral stimulation of the right hemisphere was introduced to minimize the direct effects of electrical stimulation to the brain centers of speech and memory. Controlled trials of treatments using unilateral electrode placements over 40 years have given different results. While all studies agree that the cognitive effects are less with right unilateral treatment than with bilateral treatment, some investigators conclude that the antidepressant effect is similar and others find the benefits superior for bilateral ECT (d'Elia & Raotma, 1975; Ottosson, 1991; Abrams, 2002). A recent meta-analysis, pooling the results of 22 comparative studies, finds bilateral ECT more effective than unilateral ECT (UK ECT Review Group, 2003).

The issue of whether bilateral stimulation or unilateral stimulation over the nondominant (usually right) hemisphere is preferable is mostly discussed in technical terms, although it has ethical implications. The key issue is how the principles of beneficence and non-maleficence are fulfilled, or how an optimal benefit-to-risk ratio is attained. Although the most recent meta-analysis showed a combined superiority of bilateral to unilateral stimulation, several single comparisons showed equal antidepressive efficacy. The immediate cognitive impairment was less with unilateral stimulation. Comparisons with unilateral stimulation relative to the titrated seizure threshold, however, report that the dose-response relationship extended throughout at least 12 times the seizure threshold. With improved clinical efficacy there is an increased impact on tests of memory. The high amounts of energy needed to obtain an antidepressive efficacy in unilateral ECT contrasts with the barely suprathreshold stimulation needed in bilateral ECT. The impact on anterograde amnesia was similar up to four weeks after the treatment (McCall et al., 2000). If such observations can be confirmed they challenge the view that unilateral stimulation is preferable for eliciting less cognitive disturbance. Besides, nonrandomized comparisons of similar patient series have displayed less favorable remission rates with right unilateral stimulation (Sackeim et al., 1993, 2000) compared to the recent reports of treatment with bilateral stimulation (O'Connor et al., 2001; Petrides et al., 2001). The relapse rate has also been higher with unilateral stimulation (Sackeim et al., 2001). Such evidence favors the use of bilateral over unilateral stimulation according to the severity of the underlying illness (Abrams, 2002a; Fink, 2002).

Considering the great variation of stimulus parameters, electrode placements, narcosis and concurrent medications, attempts to recommend one strategy for all clinical situations are unhelpful. As concluded by the UK ECT

Group review (2003), different clinical situations probably warrant different approaches. In a trade-off between optimally effective ECT in the elimination of depressive symptoms and minimal cognitive impairment, it is appropriate for beneficence to override nonmaleficence in the more severely ill and in those in whom there is an urgent need for symptom reduction. In such situations, bilateral stimulation is the first choice. When urgency is less, the principle of non-maleficence may get more weight, supporting the use of unilateral stimulation.

In mania, catatonia, and delirium, good outcomes are reported with bilateral stimulation. We lack experience with unilateral stimulation in patients with these illnesses, and so must rely on bilateral stimulation.

Mode of Action of ECT

A frequently stated objection to the use of ECT is that the mechanism of action is unknown. Against this may be argued that, although understanding the mechanism of action may be desirable, the decisive matter for any treatment is its efficacy and safety. ECT meets good standards on both scores and shares ignorance of its mechanism of action with many other effective and safe treatments in medicine. Research and hypotheses have been mainly focused on the antidepressant effect.

The antidepressant effect of ECT is well defined and more powerful than other antidepressant treatments. All the features of the depressive syndrome improve and not only single symptoms. Many explanations have been offered, based on the predominant view of the causes of depressive illness that was envisioned at the time. Psychological theories of the mode of the antidepressant effect (such as fear and punishment) were once prominent but these were discarded once simulated (sham) ECT was shown not to be effective. Nor is the forgetting of sad thoughts an explanation. Some memory functions improve together with the relief of depression, others deteriorate temporarily, but such memory effects are unrelated to the antidepressant effect (Cronholm & Ottosson, 1963; Fink, 1979, 1990; 2000; Abrams, 2002a)

Many authors compare the effects of ECT with the theorized effects of antidepressant drugs on the brain's neurohumors (serotonin, noradrenaline, dopamine) (Evans et al., 1976; Grahame-Smith et al., 1978; Shapira et al., 1992; Mann et al., 1996). A specific role for acetylcholine has also been pictured (Fink, 1966). These theories are mainly based on animal experiments, and when applications of the theories to man have been attempted, partial support was obtained. It is believed that antidepressant drugs facilitate humoral transmission by blocking the reuptake of neuro-transmitters in the synapses. Some authors report that ECT increases receptor sensitivity, arguing that the effect on synaptic transmission is the same as with antidepressant drugs. Others fail to confirm these findings (Fochtmann, 1994). We lack sufficient evidence to support a neurohumoral explanation based on the brain's monoamines.

Studies of the changes in the human electroencephalogram in ECT are the basis for a neurophysiologic explanation (Fink & Kahn, 1957, Abrams et al., 1972). In ECT, the interseizure EEG shows a slowing of frequencies with increased amplitudes and high voltage burst activity with increasing numbers of treatments. Measuring the changes the day after a treatment during the four weeks of ECT, the greater the degree of EEG slowing, the greater the improvement in depression. The absence of slowing was associated with poor clinical results (Fink & Kahn, 1957). Lesser degrees of slowing and an asymmetry are observed in patients treated with unilateral ECT (Volavka et al., 1973). These reports were confirmed in detailed studies reporting superior clinical outcomes in patients exhibiting greater degrees of both EEG power and postictal suppression measured by digital computer techniques (Folkerts, 1996; Nobler et al., 2000). Quantitative EEG measures also show variations in effects of different electrode placements, relative stimulus intensity, and therapeutic response (Krystal et al., 1996, 1998). Abrams (2002a) focuses attention on the generalization of the seizure (as reflected in EEG) with clinical outcome. While the association between EEG measures and clinical outcome has been well documented and even has considerable clinical relevance, an operating mechanism for this relationship has yet to be pictured.

A neuroendocrine hypothesis is more instructive and is better founded (Fink, 1999a, 2000). The hormones released by the body's endocrine glands play dominant roles in our lives, regulating growth and maturation, waking and sleeping, feeding and sex, and vigilance in daily, monthly, and lifelong cycles. They are regulated by the brain's two main hormone centers, the hypothalamus and the pituitary glands. Attention to the hormones in psychiatric illness was stimulated by the discoveries that the body's hormone functions are wildly disordered in the severe psychiatrically ill, especially in those with major depressive illnesses. One example is that the adrenal glands produce too much cortisol. The hypersecretion raises blood levels that inhibit the hypothalamus from releasing its hormones. Pituitary functions are disordered. Unhappy mood, failure to eat, loss of weight, poor sleep, loss of interest in sex, inability to concentrate thoughts, and difficulties in memory, the prominent features of depression, unfold.

An immediate large discharge of the hypothalamic hormones occurs with every seizure. In the ensuing cascade of hormonal effects, the pituitary gland discharges its products and the body's glands change their performance. The first effects are transitory, but by the fourth or fifth treatment, the normal feedback actions are again in place. Feeding and sleep become normal, and improvements in motor activity, mood, memory, and thought follow quickly.

The improved endocrine functions usually persist after an effective course of treatment, and the patient remains well. At other times, the glands revert to their abnormal activities, and a mental disorder is again evident. In such cases, repeated treatments are needed to sustain normal glandular functions and the normal mental state. Hyperactivity of the hypothalamic-pituitary-adrenocortical system is the probable cause of reduced hippocampal volume in recurrent major depression (Sheline et al., 1999; Bremner et al., 2000). In such instances, ECT restores the volume of the hippocampus which may be part of the mechanism of therapeutic action.

We have yet to identify the substances with direct effects on mood and thought that are analogous to insulin in sugar metabolism, thyroxin in cellular metabolism, and parathormone in calcium metabolism. We are optimistic that these peptide hormones will be identified and synthetic chemical substitutes will be able to replace ECT, much as we utilize replacement hormones for systemic illnesses.

The neuroendocrine view also has the possibility of being applicable to the antipsychotic and other effects of ECT since we know that the hypothalamic pituitary system discharges many hundreds of peptides into the cerebrospinal fluid and blood. It is possible that some peptides affect mood, while others affect thought, memory, and motor functions.

Summary

ECT is an effective treatment for many illnesses, often more effective than other treatments. Its efficacy compels its consideration as a treatment of the severe mentally ill.

In severe depression, ECT is effective both as a first line treatment and when antidepressant drugs fail. Since psychotic depression is usually refractory to treatment with antidepressant drugs used alone and since the risk of suicide is high, ECT should the first choice in such cases. The alternative combination of neuroleptic and antidepressant drugs has a slower onset of action and more side effects.

ECT also has an outstanding, and sometimes lifesaving, effect in other disorders, among them malignant catatonia, cycloid psychosis, acute delirium, malignant neuroleptic syndrome, postpartum psychosis, and Parkinsonism.

It is not an overstatement that ECT matches the most effective treatments in medicine. Its use complies with the ethical principle of beneficence. It may even be affirmed that withholding ECT is unethical, especially since the failure to treat a patient effectively may lead to deterioration, prolonged illness, and even death.

CHAPTER 5

Nonmaleficence

Discomforts, risks, and costs of side effects are integral parts of medical treatments and their assessment. For ECT, the side effects are few and short-lasting. It would require a much longer list to counterbalance its beneficial effects. We cannot offer such a list, despite the fact that the essence of the treatment is to induce a grand mal seizure that has potential hazards. Unlike spontaneous epileptic fits, the seizures in convulsive therapy are evoked under medically supervised conditions. A physical examination is made before the treatment to identify the care needed to minimize risks and specialists are consulted. An anesthesiologist assures full oxygenation and mitigates muscular contractions. Clinicians have so reduced the hazards of ECT that even the systemically ill, the pregnant, and the elderly-elderly can now be safely treated. Indeed, the treatment is now so lenient and the professional skills so established that only a few absolute contraindications to its use are recognized (APA, 2001; Abrams, 2002). The technique for modern ECT is markedly different from the bone-breaking, mind-numbing procedure that is pictured in popular literature and films.

Of all the anticipated risks—panic and fear of the treatment, fractures, spontaneous seizures, death, disturbed cognitive functions, and brain damage—only the effects on memory are relevant to today's practice. While the loss of memory is nearly always limited and transient, and modern treatment has developed techniques to minimize these effects further, this concern has frightened the public and the profession to become the main stumbling block to ECT's use.

Panic and Fear

Pentylenetetrazol (Metrazol) is an intravenous medication that was first used to induce a seizure. The injection was accompanied by intense feelings of impending doom and uncontrollable rapid beating of the heart, so strong as to make cooperation with later treatments almost impossible. Electrical induction produced sudden and immediate effects that obviated panic and fear. With anesthesia, the anticipatory fears were relieved. After patients experienced the first treatments, they usually return willingly for their next (Endler, 1982; Manning, 1994; Nuland, 2003; Rosenberg, 2003).

Fracture

A sudden contraction of the body may lead to fractures. Clinicians quickly learned how to use sheet restraints to reduce the contractions, but fractures still occurred. With chemical muscle relaxants, such as succinylcholine, fractures are no longer anticipated. Their exceptional occurrence is the result of a failure in the treatment technique (APA, 2001).

Spontaneous Seizures

Chemical inductions of seizures were occasionally followed by a second and even a third seizure as the medications continued to circulate in the body. These occurred within the first few hours after the treatment. Spontaneous seizures occasionally followed pentylenetetrazol, and were more common with insulin coma therapy. They are not reported with electrically induced seizures (APA, 1978).

Death

Despite anesthesia, multiple inductions of seizures, and its use in the elderly-elderly, the pregnant, and those with systemic illnesses, the mortality rate is remarkably low. The immediate mortality rate is estimated to be the same as reported for minor surgery or childbirth (APA, 1990, 2001; Abrams, 2002). In the 1980s, the incidence was estimated as 4 deaths per 100,000 treatments. The rate has decreased in recent years to 2 deaths per 100,000 treatments (or 1 per 10,000 patients) (Kramer, 1985, 1999; Abrams, 2002). Interestingly and inexplicably, longitudinal follow-up studies of depressed patients after hospitalization find the mortality rates to be lower for those treated with ECT than those treated with medications (Avery & Winokur, 1976; Prudic & Sackeim, 1999). In discussing these findings, Abrams suggests that the reduced mortality may result from the reduction in depression, although reduction in resting blood pressure may also contribute (Swartz & Inglis, 1990).

The spontaneous death rate in the age ranges of ECT samples is 4.5% per year or 1 in 195 over a 6-week interval (Glynn et al., 1995). For comparison, there is a 17-fold increase in risk of fatal myocardial infarction and 3-fold increase in the risk of subarachnoid hemorrhage in young women ages 16 to 39 years currently taking psychotropic drugs, particularly tricyclic antidepressants and benzodiazepines (Abrams, 2002).

Suicide is a leading cause of death among psychiatrically ill patients. ECT sharply reduces suicide risk. It has a rapid and immediate effect on suicidal thoughts and acts (chapter 4).

Cognitive Effects

Cognitive impairment and loss of memories are the most feared effects of ECT. The effects have been extensively studied with sophisticated neuropsychological tests. The impact on cognition has driven modern research to improve the treatment process, and this drive has been successful. Modern treatments interfere with memory for shorter durations and to a lesser degree than heretofore.

The immediate cognitive effect after each seizure is confusion that is perceived immediately on awakening. Speech is slurred, answers to questions are approximate, and orientation imperfect. The duration varies with the age and physical status of the patient, with older patients in poor physical health having the greater impairments for longer periods. Memory is also affected by the technical features of the treatment, such as the anesthetic employed, number and frequency of treatments, electrode placements, and electrical energy. These factors alter the short-term effects of treatment. The confusion that follows immediately after a seizure may be perceived for periods as short as a few minutes to many hours, but clears within a few hours in most treatments.

Memory impairment is a feature of ECT. It is confined to explicit memory—of what we are aware and can describe. Implicit memory—what we have learned or experienced—is not affected. Neither semantic (general knowledge) nor procedural memory (skills) are affected, and only occasionally, as with the patient cited as A Practicing Psychiatrist (1965) described below, is perceptual memory (recognition of sensory impressions) impacted. The characteristic disturbance after ECT concerns episodic memory, displaying both as retrograde amnesia (for events preceding the treatment) and anterograde amnesia (for events following the treatment).

These effects are most apparent immediately after each seizure, and progress in severity and duration with increasing numbers of treatments. Older patients have more severe and more prominent disturbances than younger patients, and they persist for longer periods (Sackeim, 1986, 2000).

The placing of the electrodes affects memory. Electrical stimulation applied through bitemporal electrodes shows more immediate impact than stimulation that is applied through unilateral stimulation (Sackeim, 1986, 2000; Abrams, 2002; APA, 2001). Stimulation based on sinusoidal currents causes more impairment than the brief-pulse square wave currents that are currently used (Rami-Gonzalez et al., 2001).

While the memory effects are mostly transient, the therapeutic effects are longer lasting. This dissociation between the persistence in benefits and the transience of memory effects removes memory disturbance as essential to the recovery process. Memory effects are side effects that are not in the therapeutic train.

Retrograde Amnesia

Retrograde amnesia is the recall of events that preceded the treatment. It has been examined for both personal life events and for public events, such as the recall of television programs in earlier years. Recent events are more difficult to recall than are more remote events. The events that occurred during the weeks or months of severe illness and during the weeks of treatment may be lost (Calev et al., 1991, 1995). Such difficulties of recall also occur during severe episodes of psychiatric illness in patients not treated with ECT, indicating that illness-related factors are a major cause (Calev et al., 1986, 1991). The events do not register, and therefore cannot be recalled. Recall is also impaired with tricyclic antidepressants (Calev et al., 1989). Some of the enthusiasm for the use of the SSRI and similar agents, in preference to the tricyclic drugs, is for their lesser effects on recall (Fairweather et al., 1996; Harmer et al., 2002). Indeed, some reports find memory performance to improve during treatment with SSRI antidepressants and not the earlier TCA medicines (Nowakowska et al., 1996; Levkovitz et al., 2002).

A review of 39 early studies with various tests confirmed the finding that ECT does not normally produce long-term impairment of memory. In prospective studies, subtle but persistent defects occurred several months after ECT, especially in autobiographical material. Such defects were more annoying than disabling (Taylor et al., 1982). Almost all of the studies used old-fashioned stimulation technique that causes more memory disturbance than modern brief stimulus technique.

More recent studies describe the relief of memory effects with increasing time from the ECT course. Calev and colleagues (1991), studying retrograde amnesia in depressed patients treated with brief pulse bilateral ECT, reported that the recall of personal and public events had returned to the pre-ECT level after one month. After six months it even exceeded the recall before ECT. No decrement relative to baseline, regardless of dosage and electrode placement, was observed after two months in other studies (Sackeim et al., 1993, 2000; Lisanby et al., 2000).

Anterograde Amnesia

Anterograde amnesia is the impact of treatment on the memory of events after the treatment. To understand the neuropsychological process behind anterograde amnesia after ECT, the distinction between learning (acquisition) and retention (consolidation) is useful. During a depressive illness, the ability to learn new information is impaired, probably because attention, concentration, and motivation are affected. When the depressive illness is relieved, either with ECT, medication, or spontaneously, the patient's attention, concentration, interest, and executive functions return. The treatments themselves, however, transiently impair the retention (consolidation) of memory. To argue that memory is disturbed after ECT is a half-truth; learning improves as depressed mood and disturbed thought are relieved. Patients whose illness has been marked by the severe cognitive effects described as "pseudodementia" may even display a remarkable degree of memory improvement (Roth & Rosie, 1953; Kiloh, 1961). Some patients, however, especially those not improved by the treatment, may experience the memory effects as an additional burden.

The duration of anterograde amnesia has been studied by Cronholm and coworkers (Ottosson, 1985). Bilateral ECT with 5 msec unidirectional pulses in bursts was used. Using the reproduction three hours after presentation of a word pair test the post-treatment level was 43% of the pretreatment level six hours after the first treatment, and 26% six hours after the second treatment, showing increasing impairment with additional treatments. After a complete series (2–12 treatments) the level was 47% after 4 to 5 days, 84% after a week, and 104% after a month. The authors concluded that most of the loss is regained within a week and all of it between a week and a month. With unilateral nondominant ECT, the level was 89% after 4 to 5 days, compared with 47% with bilateral ECT. Part of the memory improvement can be explained by improvement of the depressive state (Cronholm & Ottosson, 1961).

In another prospective study where sine wave stimulation was used, cognitive functions were examined in groups of ECT and non-ECT treated depressive patients. ECT caused little impairment after four months and no impairment after seven months. Being equally antidepressant, bilateral ECT caused more impairment than unilateral ECT one week after a course but the difference disappeared three months later. The authors concluded that ECT does not normally produce enduring effects on memory, and that unilateral

ECT causes very little impairment even in the short term (Weeks et al., 1980).

Subjective Memory Dysfunction

Why do some patients report that their memory is not as good as before ECT? Even with all modern precautions and with an absence of objective correlates, some patients complain of persistent memory disturbances and feelings of estrangement.

In a survey of four studies, 29 to 55 percent of the patients reported persistent or permanent memory loss after ECT (Rose et al., 2003). The interval from ECT and the parameters of the treatments (frequency, dosage, and electrode placement) were not accounted for, nor was the clinical state of the patients. One of the studies assessed volunteers obtained from advertisements asking for reports of dissatisfaction with ECT. At least three studies used outdated stimulation techniques. No conclusions for modern ECT can be drawn from this survey.

Persistent loss in memory for her skills as a government economist after a course of ECT for unrelieved dental pain and depression was reported by Marilyn Rice, the organizer of the lay anti-ECT group, the Committee for Truth in Psychiatry. Her experience is reported in the *New Yorker* essay "As Empty as Eve" (Roueché, 1974). We do not want to make light of her complaints but despite her claims of inability to work, she was able to write and document knowingly about the literature on the brain consequences of ECT and to organize and lead an active membership organization.

Donahue (2000), a lawyer, received ECT for a severe depressive illness. She recovered and has carried on an active law practice. She writes about the effects on memory:

> Occassionally, I feel bitter. More often, it is a sadness, a sense of a deep loss that may not even have had to happen. It is a grief that keeps deepening over time, because there is hardly a week that goes by that I do not discover yet another part of my life that is lost somewhere in my memory cells.
>
> Despite that, I remain unflagging in my belief that the electroconvulsive therapy that I received in the fall of 1995 and then the spring of 1996—33 treatments, initially unilateral and then bilateral—may have saved not just my mental health, but my life. If I had the same decision to make over again, I would choose ECT over a life condemned to psychic agaony, and possible suicide. (p. 133)

Opposite testimonies of other knowledgeable persons who have undergone ECT may contribute to a balanced view on the clinical significance of

glutamate/glutamine, known as stimulatory transmitter substances. After successful ECT the levels were normalized and did not differ from healthy age- and sex-matched controls (Pfleiderer et al., 2003).

Summary

The risks of ECT have changed markedly in the many decades of its use. The panic and fear of treatments, fractures, and severe confusion that marked its early years have been attenuated by technical improvements. Anesthesia and muscle relaxation have almost obliterated fractures, and changes in technical features of energy form, placement of electrodes, numbers and frequency of treatments, and dosing have alleviated cognitive effects. The risk of death is very small. Brain imaging has not disclosed signs of damage; on the contrary, growth of neurons is stimulated.

The principal objection is the anticipation of impaired memory. While all seizures are accompanied by short periods of confusion, memory disturbances are usually restricted to a gap for the time of psychiatric illness and treatment, which also occurs when ECT has not been given. Prolonged memory losses, so much discussed, are uncommon but complaints occasionally occur about impaired recollection of personal and public events, as well as forgetfulness in daily living. The role of ECT in these events is uncertain.

When, as in most cases, there is no or only temporary memory impairment which is experienced as a nuisance rather than a handicap, modern ECT is consistent with the ethical principle of non-maleficence. When, as occasionally reported, there is a handicapping memory impairment, the nonmaleficence principle has not been fulfilled. In some instances the relief of a severe mental illness may outweigh the cognitive impairment, in others that is not the case. Different opinions on the role of ECT in the memory complaints prevail among patients and the psychiatric profession.

CHAPTER 6
Autonomy

Autonomy implies respect for an individual's decisions about personal care. In view of the asymmetry between an individual's limited medical knowledge and that of professionals, traditional medicine supported a paternalistic attitude in which the decisions were made by the knowledgeable professional without specific roles for patients. As Western democracies extolled the merits of individual decisions, a respect for patient autonomy rose. Autonomous decisions require understanding, maturity, responsibility, and discernment. Since these human properties are disturbed in psychiatric disorders, often severely so, the question is raised: How far is it possible to respect autonomy in treating the mentally ill?

Competence and Rationality

The division into two stages of competence, that of competent and incompetent, and the subdivision of decision-making into rational and irrational are starting points for analysis. While incompetent patients cannot make valid decisions, opinions differ on the dividing line between rationality and irrationality. A particular problem is how seemingly irrational reasoning of the competent patient should be treated.

Culver and coworkers (1980) accept the failure of a competent patient to consent even when the thinking is clearly irrational. They endorse abstention from ECT even on irrational grounds, a distinction which, in our opinion, is too permissive. When delusions govern the refusal (e.g., "not the wish of God," "I am sinful," "I am not worthy of treatment," "I deserve to die"), the decision is not being made voluntarily. In such instances, the minimal criteria of Culver and coworkers are not sufficient; the complimentary qualification that the patient must not have a distorted reality perception needs to be added.

We are sympathetic to the views expressed in an editorial of the *Journal of Medical Ethics* (1983). Individuals under the influence of a psychosis do not have the same perceptions of reality as they have when they are healthy. Accordingly, if a patient refuses ECT under the influence of perceptional or delusional distortions of a psychotic state, ECT may be instituted against the patient's wishes. The principle of beneficence overrides respect for autonomy.

Paternalism versus Authoritarianism

In a review of the ethics of electroconvulsive therapy and other somatic treatments, the Canadian psychiatrist Merskey (1999) adopts a paternalistic position. Just as it is valuable for children to have good parents, a good paternal (or maternal) physician can be valuable to psychotic patients. It is not necessary to reject paternalism totally because it is sometimes confused with authoritarianism. Incompetent patients have a right to the most effective treatment, be it ECT or any other. Physicians have the obligation to save life even if it means overriding a patient's wishes. A justification is often seen when patients are grateful after recovery. Doctors who refrain from ECT when the indications are satisfied could be regarded as morally, even if not legally, negligent.

We agree with Merskey. Paternalism is acting as good parents as long as patients cannot decide for themselves. Authoritarianism, on the other hand, reflects insensitiveness, the disrespect for patient autonomy and integrity, and the lust for power.

Such a view does not justify, nor does it encourage, coercive methods to accomplish treatment. If a good interpersonal relationship has been established between the patient and the professional staff and sufficient time is devoted to educate the patient and family members, psychotic patients may come to understand that the recommended treatment is aimed at alleviating their distress. With a confident patient-doctor relationship, even delusional patients may accept a proposed intervention.

Although we have worked in different health care cultures, we have seldom met individuals who fail to consent to ECT, even when they are severely depressed. We recommend ECT when other treatments have failed or the indications for primary treatment are so clear that we are convinced that ECT is justified.

Irrational Refusal

Nonpsychotic patients who have not responded to antidepressant drugs and suffer severely may give seemingly irrational reasons for declining ECT ("afraid of dying," "losing memory," "barbaric treatment"). When life is not at stake, we accept the patient's opinion even when the reasons are irrational. Alternative treatments are offered and if not successful, we try to persuade the patient to accept ECT, eventually with the assistance of well-informed relatives or successfully treated patients.

Irrational Consent

Psychotic patients may consent for irrational reasons ("deserve to be punished or executed"). Since they are consenting to receive an appropriate treatment, and since the alternative of refraining from treatment would leave them in the psychotic state, we do not have misgivings about accepting such consent.

Written Consent

It may be too much to insist on a signed, written consent. A nod of understanding and cooperation for the treatment as personnel meet no objection when preparing the patient should be acceptable. The insistence on a signed written consent encourages distrust and disturbs the delicate relationship between the patient and the psychiatrist. Yet, as the signed consent has become a standard of care in the United States and some other cultures, we accept this intervention as promoting better care.

We present an example of a depressed psychotic patient who refused to sign a written form for consent, yet who cooperated for a successful treatment course.

ACQUIESCENCE, NOT CONSENT

A 68-year-old scientist had not graciously accepted his retirement three years earlier. Self-sufficient, he had few friends and his work had been the main interest in his life. He was married but had no children. Six months earlier, his wife had become bed-ridden, unable to manage their home.

He grew despondent, ate poorly thinking that his food was poisoned, slept during much of the day, was up much of the night, bathed irregularly, and complained of constipation, of abdominal, back, and neck pains. He insisted, contrary to fact, that he had heart disease and would soon die. He accused his wife of infidelity and refused to talk to her. He believed his neighbors were spying on his home, and watched the street from behind curtained windows for hours at a time.

When the patient was brought to the hospital by an aide, he was unkempt and disheveled, walked slowly. He had an unpleasant body odor, refused to answer questions, and was reluctant to let the doctors examine him. He accused them of plotting to steal his money. He insisted that he was physically ill, that his condition was hopeless, and that treatment would be of no avail. At times, he appeared to be hearing voices and muttering barely audible responses.

Clinical and laboratory examinations showed no signs of systemic disease other than eczema and dermatitis resulting from poor skin care. The patient's kidney functions were impaired because he had been drinking too little. Intravenous fluids and feeding were started.

He refused medications, insisting that treatment was pointless, as death was imminent, but his symptoms convinced the doctors that he needed immediate treatment. When they described the risks and benefits of ECT, he listened carefully, read the consent form, and then declared that he would not sign it. His wife, with whom the course of ECT was discussed, did agree to the husband's treatment. The medical director, having noted the severity of the illness, the delusional content of the patient's thoughts, the severe inanition and dehydration, poor self-care, and refusal to take medications, also recommended ECT. Although he refused to sign a formal consent, he allowed the staff to examine him and to administer intravenous fluids, so it seemed reasonable to offer him ECT.

The next morning, he put on his pajamas and came willingly to the treatment room. Again, the procedures were explained, and he was asked to move onto the stretcher. Although he pointed out that he had not signed the consent, he cooperated fully with instructions. An intravenous line was established, monitoring electrodes and blood pressure cuffs applied, and anesthesia given. During all subsequent treatments he cooperated in the same fashion. These were given three times a week with bilateral electrode placement, and effective seizures were elicited. He soon began to drink and eat, returned to a normal sleep cycle, and showed a greater interest in his personal care. He showered when asked to, took his meals in the common room, applied the medications prescribed for his skin, and drank fluids as requested. He did not, however, take the prescribed oral medications. His delusional thoughts persisted.

After 12 treatments, he was no longer sure that his wife was unfaithful—indeed, he was sympathetic to her—and was puzzled as he recollected his thoughts about the neighbors. After 15 treatments, he was sufficiently improved to go home, and he was advised to continue ECT on a weekly basis for two more months.

When he was discharged, his mood improved, he had gained 15 pounds in weight, attended to his bodily care, remained puzzled by the stories of his strange thoughts, and went home to care for his wife. During a friendly exchange as he was leaving the hospital, he pointed out that he had never signed the consent for treatment and asked, with a smile, whether the psychiatrist would lose his license as a result. He had accepted treatment, he said, because he believed that his condition was hopeless and that he had no reason not to be a "good guy" and cooperate.

One year later, he had maintained his weight, was sleeping well, and his illness had not recurred.

(Fink, 1999)

Compulsory Treatment

Compulsory treatment is rarely needed but in some venues, as in some of the United States, regulations provide for an application to a court for an adjudicated consent. Courts usually require evidence that the life of the patient (as by suicide) or that of others may be harmed if treatment is not provided. In Sweden, compulsory treatment can be given to patients without court mandate provided they are in compulsory institutional care. When patients have recovered, they are often grateful for their recovery. As patients improve, many consent to further treatments.

Catatonia: A Unique Problem in Consent

A particularly complex issue in assuring voluntary consent is seen in patients who develop catatonia. Mutism, negativism, rigidity, and posturing are salient characteristics that preclude individual consent to treatment. Catatonia is a life-threatening illness, especially in its malignant forms. At the same time, it is remarkably responsive to medications, especially intravenous barbiturates and benzodiazepines, and when these fail, to ECT (Fink & Taylor, 2003). In the usual care of such patients, medications are prescribed without specific consent of the patient. When the medications fail and ECT is indicated, the requirement for a voluntary signed consent becomes an extraordinary hurdle. The following report exemplifies the difficulty and argues for a unique way to assure consent.

CONSENT IN CATATONIA

A young adult soldier in a catatonic state faced possible death from inanition. His relatives were not known and advanced directives were not available. The jurisdiction in which he had become ill (Texas) forbade substituted judgment for ECT and a curative course could not be given without consent. He had been brought to medical attention because he was bewildered, unable to carry out his duties, and responded with few monosyllabic answers to inquiries. After the administration of intramuscular lorazepam, he was able to give additional history, complained of confusion, and expressed fear that he could not speak normally. Within two hours he again became unresponsive, moved little, and exhibited posturing, waxy flexibility, and negativism.

Since the use of benzodiazepines provided only transient relief, it was decided that ECT was the only effective remedy. To obtain the patient's consent, he was given intravenous lorazepam (3 mg). His catatonic state dissipated, he sat up, began to cry, and related that he missed his parents and believed that he was "going crazy." He described his condition and implored the examiners not to allow him to revert to his state of confusion and its perceptual distortions.

During the next two hours, three psychiatrists separately assessed his ability to consent to ECT. The examiners agreed that he demonstrated, at least temporarily, the necessary understanding and judgment to consent to ECT. He was treated with ECT over four weeks with adjunctive risperidone and fluoxetine, responded well, and was discharged to his parents' care. The discharge diagnosis was bipolar disorder. The illness meets the criteria for delirious mania, a subtype of catatonic disorders (Fink, 1999; Fink and Taylor, 2003).

At follow-up three months later, he was living with his parents, employed full time, euthymic and not psychotic.

(Bostwick & Chozinski, 2002)

Mental Retardation

Another special problem is presented by mentally retarded patients with comorbid psychiatric illness. By their lack of understanding, such patients are incompetent to make valid decisions about their care. An independent second opinion by a person experienced in both ECT and mental retardation could be an ethically sound basis for paternalistic intervention. It is made in the best interest of the patient and need not be associated with loss of liberty or coercion. A survey of such cases shows successful outcomes, both acutely and in continuation and maintenance treatment. Too often ECT is delayed and left as a treatment of last choice (Little et al., 2002).

Summary

Respect for autonomy is a basic ethical principle in health care. Given sufficient time and patience, even severely depressed patients with delusions are able to consent to ECT, in words, in body language, or by not resisting when being prepared for the treatment. The unexceptional request for written consent may be an inconvenient impediment. It may be even more of an unnecessary impediment when patients are asked to sign individual consent

seen when any potential treatment for HIV-infection is announced. A particularly relevant example is seen in the history of clozapine, an antipsychotic medication of high risk, high expense, and marginal advantage over established antipsychotic drugs. When its benefits were defined in experimental studies, the expense was deemed too high for the limited benefit. Yet, when the public was assured that for some patients the marginal advantage would be meaningful, an outcry led state legislatures in the United States to authorize the expenditure, even at the expense of competing interests.

United States

Availability of ECT is uneven. Many hospitals and clinics licensed to treat the mentally ill are not equipped to deliver ECT. It is hardly an excuse that the variability is better documented than in many other nations.

Few psychiatrists are skilled in ECT. In a survey of the members of the American Psychiatric Association in 1988, less than 8% provided this service (Hermann et al., 1998). They were predominantly male, more likely to have graduated from a medical school outside the United States, and to have received their psychiatric training in the 1960s or 1980s, rather than the 1970s. They were also more likely to practice at private rather than state or county public hospitals.

In the same survey data, the respondents had treated patients in 202 Metropolitan areas, leaving 115 regions without reported experience (Hermann et al., 1995). Annual ECT use varied from 0.4 to 81.2 patients per 10,000 population. Greater numbers of patients were treated in the communities with the larger number of both psychiatrists and primary care physicians in a metropolitan district. Use was also greater with higher numbers of private hospital beds per capita and greater in those venues with the least restrictive state regulation of ECT.

In assessing ECT in Medicare beneficiaries, a small increase in use and in outpatient treatments occurred between 1987 and 1992 (Rosenbach et al., 1997). The increase was greater among women and whites under age of 65, than among males, nonwhites, and the elderly. The expenditures for outpatient ECT increased from 7% in 1987 to 16% in 1992.

A survey of ECT use from a large New England insurance company in 1994–1995 found the diagnosis was within evidence-based indications for 86.5% of the courses of ECT. In more than half of the rest, the indications were for the relief of depressive mood disorders (Hermann et al., 1999).

Few state, federal, or Veterans Administration hospitals provide ECT, and where it is available, its use is infrequent (Thompson et al., 1987, 1994). More than 60% of the patients were treated in private general and psychiatric hospitals. While 8 to 12% of adult inpatients at academic hospitals receive ECT, less than 0.2% of adults at nonacademic centers get its benefits (Thompson et al., 1994). Fewer African Americans with affective disorders receive ECT than Caucasian Americans (Breakey & Dunn, in press).

The discrepancies in availability of ECT in the United States are probably a reflection of the continuing social stigma and bias against the treatment. Before the Medicare and Hill-Burton legislative acts of the 1960s opened access for U.S. patients to any hospital facility, such discrepancies were common. After the nation adopted an open-admission policy to its psychiatric facilities, encouraging patients of all social classes to seek admission and help in the hospitals nearest their homes, such discrepancies are no longer justified.

An example of poor treatment is seen in an academic institution that did not have ECT available for its patients.

FAILURE TO TREAT FOR LACK OF ECT FACILITY

A 40-year-old man had been treated for psychosis with antipsychotic and anti-manic medications since age sixteen. He was attending a community clinic, and was stabilized with lithium and chlorpromazine therapy. Encouraged by the stability of his condition, his therapist prescribed olanzapine, then a new atypical antipsychotic. Within a few weeks, the patient again became psychotic. Perphenazine was prescribed and within a day he became febrile, mute, and rigid. He was hospitalized, the diagnosis of a neuroleptic malignant syndrome was made, and he was transferred to a tertiary care medical facility.

Antipsychotic medications were discontinued and he was treated with large doses of bromocriptine and dantrolene. Repetitive motor movements erroneously prompted the diagnosis of epilepsy, so anticonvulsants were administered. Lorazepam, prescribed in low doses, controlled infrequent agitation. He remained mute and rigid and required total nursing care. After a few weeks, he was unable to stand; his hands and legs were in a rigid, immobile posture. A gastrostomy was done to permit feeding. He developed pulmonary and bladder infections requiring antibiotics.

After he had been in intensive medical care for four months, a visiting consultant recommended lorazepam at high doses. When the daily dose was increased to 12 mg, the patient responded to commands and smiled at his parents, though he remained mute. ECT was recommended, but the hospital did not have this facility available, so he was transferred to one that could. When his mother was signing the consent for ECT on behalf of her son, she recalled that he had a similar episode of rigidity, mutism, and psychosis when he was 16 years of age. He had responded well to ECT.

Lorazepam was reduced to 6 mg/day and bilateral ECT was begun. After 4 treatments, he recognized his parents, vocalized, smiled, was less rigid, and took oral feedings. By the ninth treatment, he was verbally responsive, but the four months of rigidity and forced bed rest had left him with limb contractures and such badly impaired movement that he was unable to stand or to use his hands to feed himself. Both catatonia and psychosis were relieved. After 22 ECT, he was transferred to a rehabilitation center and four months later he was again able to walk, use his hands, and care for himself.

(Fink & Taylor, 2003)

For lack of experience with ECT, the professional staff did not institute the proper treatment for neuroleptic malignant syndrome, allowing the patient to develop severe contractures. Had a consultant not seen him and made the proper diagnosis, the patient would have fared much less well.

We have detailed data on the use of ECT in California and Texas, two states where the law requires the reporting of all ECT administered in non-Federal hospitals. In California, from 1977 to 1994, the mean rate of use was 0.90 patients/10,000 population, similar to earlier rates (Kramer, 1999) and contrasting with an estimated national rate of 4.9/10,000 (Hermann et al., 1995). Less than six percent of the patients received ECT in public hospitals, being available in only one state hospital. White and Asian patients received 91.5% of the treatments, with black patients at 2.1% and Hispanic 3.8%. This proportion is inconsistent with the distribution of ethnic groups in the population which is cited by the U.S. Census Bureau as 58% white and Asian, 32% Hispanic, and 6.4% black. Kramer writes:

> ECT is not a treatment forced on minority groups or the poor. On the contrary, ECT is less available for public patients.... The excuse that stringent laws are needed to protect the patient is no longer valid. (p. 249)

Less than 3% of the patients were incapable of giving voluntary consent and received ECT after court review.

About 6% of Texas psychiatrists performed ECT at 50 hospitals between 1993 and 1995, with only one state facility offering the treatment (Reid et al., 1998). Of the patients receiving ECT, 88% were white in a state in which the 55% of the residents are white, 32% Hispanic, and 11% black. Virtually all patients were deemed capable of consenting to ECT including committed-but-consenting patients. Although Texas law deems any deaths within fourteen days, regardless of cause, as related to ECT, no deaths could be related to the treatment.

In the procedures in which psychiatric insurers allow payments for psychiatric treatment, ECT is an option that comes late in the course of the illness, usually after more than one medication trial has failed. Such an attitude makes it impossible for the managed care insurers, including Medicare and Medicaid, to do other than ignore ECT or to relegate it to the treatment of suicidal patients or those who have suffered far too long.

Canada

The Province of Quebec requested an assessment of ECT by its Agence d'Evaluation des Technologies et des Modes d'Intervention en Santé in response to public pressures to limit its use. An extensive 2003 report highlights its controversial nature (AETMIS, 2002). Between 1988 and 1996, ECT use increased from 4,000 to 7,200 annual treatments and thereafter remained flat. The number of treatment sessions per 1,000 population is comparable to that reported in California and England, but only 40% of the rate in Ontario (Canada) and 25% of the rate in Denmark and the East Anglia District in England. The number of out-patient administrations increased markedly. Low reimbursement rates hamper its use in Canada, as well as in other countries.

United Kingdom

Availability of ECT in the United Kingdom is comparable to that in the United States. A survey of U.K. practice found meeting the guidelines of the Royal College of Psychiatrists difficult (Brookes et al., 2000). A national audit of ECT in Scotland between 1997 and 2000 showed that the annual rate of ECT was 16 courses per 10,000 population, given mainly to white adult patients with a depressive illness. Clinical improvement, assessed as a 50% reduction in a standard rating scale for depression, was evident in 71% of patients with depression (SEAN, 2002). A recent review of ECT as part of the National Health Service technology assessment program finds that

> ... despite substantial advances in safety and technique, including routine use
> of electroencephalogram monitoring, ECT is also one of the most clinically
> neglected treatments in psychiatry. (Eranti & McLoughlin, 2003, p. 8)

The use of ECT is declining in the United Kingdom with widespread variability in standards and practice. They cite a report that found an 18-fold difference in use between 11 general adult psychiatric teams within a single

Edinburgh teaching hospital (Glen & Scott, 2000). Another audit found up to a 12-fold difference in use between centers (Pippard, 1992). Despite the educational activities of the Royal College of Psychiatrists, little progress was found in follow-up; only one-third had established suitable policies to assist doctors in ECT (Duffett & Lelliott, 1998). A survey of 230 ECT facilities in 2000–2001 found substantial departures from best treatment standards (Mental Health Act Commission, 2001). The authors reflect that such inconsistencies are not limited to the United Kingdom but are found in many other countries. In conclusion, the authors suggest a national policy of monitoring and accrediting ECT clinics as satisfying RCP guidelines for best practice and safety. As an alternative, they suggest that regional specialist centers be developed to assure expertise in ECT.

Nordic Countries

ECT is given in all the Nordic countries, more so in Denmark and Sweden than in Norway, Finland, and Iceland. A survey in Sweden in 1992 to 1993 showed that 12.6 per 10,000 inhabitants were given ECT annually (National Board of Health and Welfare, 1994). Treatments were given in all counties but there was an eight-fold variation. Areas with higher use of ECT also had a higher consumption of antidepressant drugs and lithium. The major indications were severe and drug-refractory depression, and in other depressive states, cycloid and puerperal psychoses. ECT was not used in children, adolescents, or in forensic patients. Most treatments were given after informed consent with 1.8% receiving treatments against their wishes and another 4.8% had the first treatment involuntarily and the rest with voluntary consent. A Swedish patient may not appeal a treatment decision, but only the compulsory admission. Most patients accepted ECT when it was proffered. Side effects were rarely reported. On the whole, the attitudes to ECT were positive among psychiatrists. Nearly all considered that training in the use of ECT should be available and most had received formal training. Few Swedish psychiatrists say that they would refuse ECT if they themselves had a drug-resistant depression with melancholic features. ECT belongs in specialist training as the same matter of course as psychotherapy and psychopharmacology. The practice is similar in other Scandinavian countries.

In all Nordic countries unilateral and combined unilateral-bilateral ECT had increased and exclusively bilateral ECT decreased between 1977 and 1987 (Strömgren, 1991). In 1999, 5% of all hospitalized patients received ECT in Denmark, but there was a five-fold variation between the hospitals, ascribed to different treatment traditions (Andersson & Bolwig, 2002). The authors reported a 17% decrease in number of ECT sessions and a decrease in patients of 27% from 1979 to 1999, suggesting that treatment courses were longer in 1999.

Rest of Europe

In Germany, Italy, Austria, and the Netherlands, use is limited, although recent reports show increasing usage. It is available only in specialist centers in Belgium and Germany, or limited by the unavailability of anesthetic services, equipment, or trained staff in Poland, Latvia, Spain, and Romania (Philpot et al., 2002). Some cantons in Switzerland and the national governments in Italy and Slovenia limit its use. In France, there is a similar maldistribution of facilities but an increase in maintenance ECT is reported (Benadhira & Teles, 2001). The authors state:

> Last but not least, the proper equipment for practicing ECT seems to be sadly lacking in many of the psychiatric wards. This brings further to the fore the debate, so common in France, regarding the equal distribution of the availability of all medical care to each and every citizen wherever he may be living. (p. 129)

In Italy, where ECT was first developed, its use is almost completely banned in public psychiatric hospitals, psychiatric wards in general hospitals, and in university departments (Koukopoulos, 1993). At the time, it was given in only 4 of 49 university wards. On the other hand, ECT was used in most of the 68 private psychiatric hospitals, but without much public attention. Those few psychiatrists who administered ECT in public institutions have received admonitions from the State Health Unit and were told that it is "politically inopportune." Yet, the majority of Italian psychiatrists are in favor of its use. The attitude of patients and their families is also much less negative than the attitudes of politicians.

The Netherlands guidelines consider ECT a treatment of choice in depressive disorders with psychotic features, severe suicidal behavior, severe physical exhaustion or resistance to treatment with two or more antidepressants. It is also advised to use ECT early in depressed elderly where drugs may have troublesome side effects. Despite these recommendations, ECT use is infrequent, as reported in a mail questionnaire survey (van der Wurff et al., 2004). A majority of Dutch psychiatrists had strongly reserved opinions to consider ECT as recommended by the official guidelines. The authors speculate that the attitudes are remnants from the tumultuous 1970s when the Dutch polity expressed strong negative opinions toward medical and biological perspectives in psychiatry. The survey was addressed to psychiatrists over the age of 65; the attitudes among younger psychiatrists were not studied.

Australia and New Zealand

A detailed review of the use of ECT in young people between 1990 and 1996 undertaken by Rey and Walter (1997) and Walter and Rey (1997) found that although the efficacy in adolescents and children is similar to that in adults, ECT is rarely used. Less than 1% of the patients treated with ECT were under the age of 19 years. A survey of the attitudes of child and adolescent psychiatrists found their knowledge of ECT inadequate, despite the fact that the respondents averred an interest in using ECT (Walter et al., 1997). In a survey of 26 interviewed adolescent recipients of ECT, the respondents expressed positive recollections of their ECT experience and more than half thought ECT had been helpful (Walter et al., 1999).

Another Australian survey of ECT reported usage rates comparable to those in the United States (Wood & Burgess, 2003). A questionnaire survey in New Zealand found that many psychiatrists acknowledged the British Royal College guidelines but used them less frequently. In particular, New Zealand psychiatrists reported many more conditions as "absolute contraindications" than did the RCP guidelines (Strachan, 2001).

Hong Kong

A territory-based survey of ECT in 1999 to 2000 found ECT to be available in eight of 13 inpatient psychiatric facilities (Chung & Cheung, 2003). Only three of the units met U.K. guidelines for ECT (Royal College of Psychiatrists, 1989). The number of ECT courses per 100 acute hospital beds ranged from zero to 83.8. The overall rate of ECT use was 0.34 courses per 10,000 population.

Developing Countries

The unavailability of modern equipment, the expense of the medicines for anesthesia and shortage of anesthesiologists affect the practice of ECT in many countries. When ECT is given, it is without oxygenation, anesthesia, and muscular relaxation, a procedure as in the early years of its development. Such procedures are now termed "unmodified ECT." An interesting expression of these social factors is to be seen in India in 2002 where one of us (MF) met many psychiatrists who asked about the propriety and safety of unmodified ECT. The nation lacks a national health scheme and the cost of an anesthesiologist, a hospital setting, and the medications is too high for many of the patients treated outside the major medical centers. As a consequence, practitioners either use unmodified ECT, or must forgo the benefits of the treatment.

An Indian professor of psychiatry has appealed to the Indian Supreme Court to enjoin the use of unmodified ECT (Andrade et al., 2003). MF expressed the opinion that while modified ECT is to be preferred as safer for patients, the hazards of unmodified ECT were still small and it was preferable to use unmodified ECT against no ECT at all. Instead of prohibition it would be better for academic leaders to encourage the wider use of ECT with public support of the services and medicines needed for modified ECT. One can hardly imagine that surgical patients in India are treated without anesthesia or that they do not enjoy the benefits of Western medicine.

Abstaining from ECT as Malpractice

"Right-to-treatment" litigation in the United States articulates patients' rights to be treated effectively (Stone, 1979). In Sweden, the Health and Medical Services Act prescribes that "the aim of health care is good health and care on equal terms for the entire population." Complaints about incorrect treatment are dealt with by The National Board of Health and Welfare or The Medical Responsibility Board, the latter with authority to impose disciplinary punishment in the form of admonition, warning, or striking off the medical register. ECT is regarded as an essential psychiatric treatment, based on solid evidence. The following case illustrates a disciplinary judgment.

ABSTAINING FROM ECT AS MALPRACTICE

The national disciplinary board of health care received complaints from a wife about the treatment of her husband. He was 60 years old and had been admitted to a psychiatric department for depression of melancholic type. On two previous occasions he had been successfully treated for the same disorder with ECT. This time he was first treated as an outpatient with paroxetine, a selective serotonin reuptake inhibitor (SSRI). After admission the medication was changed to moclobemide, a MAO-inhibitor, and then to a combination of paroxetine, moclobemide and a small dose of amitriptyline. The state of the patient deteriorated and his answers to questions about death and suicide were evasive. ECT was considered but was not performed. Fifteen days after admission, the patient committed suicide by hanging during a casual leave from the hospital.

The disciplinary board expressed the opinion that the continual changes of ineffective medications were likely to have caused disappointment and alarm of the patient. Suicide is always an imminent danger in melancholic depression. ECT should have been the treatment of choice at an early stage. The conclusion was that the responsible psychiatrist had not acted according to science and experience. The sanction was a warning, a more severe criticism than admonition.

(National Responsibility Board, 1996).

Prejudices against ECT in the Elderly

ECT is effective in elderly patients; indeed the degree of improvement is often greater and more rapid than the benefits in younger adults (O'Conner et al., 2001). Patients in this age group often tolerate antidepressant drugs badly. Nevertheless, many psychiatrists hesitate to advise the use of ECT when they consider the variety and multiplicity of somatic ailments in elderly people. One even meets the opinion that ECT cannot be given above a certain age.

The task of psychiatric care is to provide all patients with the care they need and from which they can be expected to benefit. In considering the role of age in medical care, a distinction needs to be made between chronological and biological age. Chronological age is decided by birth date, while biological age depends on the conditions of the body and its organs. Chronological age can be determined exactly while biological age is a vague concept but still amenable to medical assessment.

In principle, chronological age limits must not be applied to decisions concerning examinations or treatments. What matters is whether a patient, irrespective of age, can safely be the subject of medical measures which are judged to be beneficial. Modern ECT is a lenient treatment and with proper supervision, the burden of a course of ECT is less than that of the psychiatric illness for which it is used or long lasting medication with psychotropic drugs. The principal risk in ECT is considered the impairment of memory, and although elderly people have a lower pretreatment memory level, they do not suffer greater (or more long-lasting) memory disturbance than younger people. (Ottosson, 1970; d'Elia & Raotma, 1977). Depleted physiological resources of the central nervous system, however, as evidenced by a low confusion threshold, may make special precautions necessary, *that is,* careful control of energy dosing, oxygenation, and greater intervals between the treatments.

An example is to be seen in one of the many elderly patients treated in an active ECT service.

ECT IN PRESENCE OF MEDICAL ILLNESS

A 78-year-old man was cared for at his home by his wife when he progressively developed depressed mood, a slovenly appearance, and thoughts that life was no longer worth living. He was being treated for diabetes, cardiac failure, visual difficulties, and arthritis. He lost weight and took to his bed, reluctant to leave it except for toileting. He refused medical care, asserting that the time to end his life had come. He accepted medications for his cardiac illness and diabetes reluctantly.

Medical examination showed an unshaven, unkempt man, frail and breathing with difficulty, responding to questions with single words. He was hospitalized over his objection and was bed-ridden in the hospital, requiring full nursing care. Antidepressant drugs were prescribed but after 10 days and no relief, a consultation for ECT was arranged. The consultant found the patient suffering from a major depressive illness and agreed to treat him with ECT. The medical consultant demurred, however, saying that the risks in a man with diabetes and heart failure were too severe and that the patient could not tolerate the treatment. After discussions with the family, his wife consented to his treatment, accepting the risks offered by the internist. The patient consented to treatment.

ECT was begun and after three treatments, the patient ate voluntarily, left his bed, shaved, and no longer refused medication. After five ECT, he was fully ambulatory and returned home. Continuation ECT for the next month resulted in recovery of his depressive illness and improvement in the level of his physical activity.

(Fink)

Demented patients with superimposed depression may also profit from ECT. They get more benefit from ECT than from antidepressant drugs which often have unpleasant side effects. Such patients mostly need maintenance treatment at individually appropriate intervals.

Prejudices against ECT in Young People

A similar hesitation is met in considering ECT in children and adolescents. It is almost never used to treat prepubertal children and infrequently to treat adolescents. When ECT is considered, it is almost exclusively as a last resort, after months of trials of less effective agents (Walter & Rey, 1997; Rey & Walter, 1997; Cohen et al., 2000a). One concern is that the developing brain may be damaged by electricity and seizures. Another is the prejudiced opinion that depression in the young must have a psychosocial and not a biological basis. In at least three of the states of the United States, legislation restricts the use of ECT in adolescents. These concerns discourage the consideration of ECT even when antidepressant drugs and psychotherapy have no effect.

Whereas ECT-responsive illnesses seldom begin before puberty, their prevalence increases during adolescence. Assessments of ECT in adolescents find the efficacy to be similar to that in adults. Patients with major depression, psychotic depression, catatonia, and excited mania respond well, reducing suicide risk and duration of illness (Walter & Rey, 1997; Cohen et al., 1997, 1999; Taieb et al., 2002). In a long-term follow-up of cognition in 10 adolescents successfully treated with ECT, no measurable impairment in cognition was observed (Cohen et al., 2000a). No ethical reasons to ban the use of ECT in adolescents are discerned in a careful analysis by Cohen and colleagues (2000b). A long-term follow-up of adolescents treated with ECT compared to matched controls found no difference in school achievement or social functioning (Taieb et al., 2002). Adolescent patient and parent attitudes to courses of ECT found overall positive attitudes in long-term follow-up (Taieb et al., 2001).

ECT is also underutilized in young people with catatonia where prejudices that psychological factors must underlie this syndrome have led to the description of a pervasive refusal syndrome (Lask et al., 1991). The report that catatonic patients have been treated with psychotherapy alone for months and years is evidence of disregard for the proper and ethical treatment of these patients (Graham & Foreman, 1995). Such treatment has been criticized as a denial of proper care (Fink & Klein, 1995). The pervasive refusal syndrome is clearly a type of catatonia and eminently treatable by benzodiazepines or ECT (Fink & Taylor, 2003).

Many examples of successful treatment of adolescents with severe psychiatric illnesses are in the literature. One such example follows.

ECT IN ADOLESCENT

A 17-year-old boy developed acute confusion after a weekend of partying. For two weeks he refused to go to school, slept and ate little, and closeted himself in his room, listening to rock music. At times, he became excited and shouted at his parents, and after three weeks they brought him to a community hospital. He was unclean, talking continuously, singing, and beating rhythms with his hands. Sedation with oral lorazepam proved inadequate and restraints were used. After two doses of haloperidol, he developed fever, rigidity, elevated blood pressure, and a rapid heart rate. He was treated with intravenous fluids and dantrolene. The febrile reaction was muted but he remained psychotic and manic and was transferred to an academic tertiary care psychiatric unit.

On admission, he was restless and confused, with slurred and disorganized speech. Consciousness waxed and waned. He told of having strange powers; that his parents, who accompanied him and were present, were not his real parents; and that he had been selected for a spectacularly successful career in finance. Although he seemed oriented to time, place, and person, he could not recall the names of three objects after five minutes. His ability to do simple numerical calculations was poor and he was unaware of notable current events. His temperature, heart rate, and blood pressure were normal. He was seen to be suffering from an acute delirious mania.

ECT was recommended. The parents agreed and despite his excitement, the patient signed consent. All medications except lithium were discontinued. On the fourth hospital day, he was given bitemporal ECT, an adequate seizure was induced, and recovery was uneventful. Within an hour, he was rational and oriented, neither overactive nor delusional, and no longer in need of restraint. Later that afternoon, however, he relapsed to his manic state and after each of the next two treatments he followed the same pattern. After the fourth treatment his thoughts, mood, and affect were appropriate, his delusional ideas had disappeared, his self-care was normal, and he remained well. He was discharged after the sixth treatment with a prescription for biweekly outpatient ECT and continuation treatment with lithium. He received four additional treatments. He returned to school, and quickly made up the work that he had missed. Lithium therapy was sustained for four months and then discontinued. He was discharged from the clinic as recovered, and was well at two month follow-up.

(Fink & Taylor, 2003)

To judge from its efficacy and safety, ECT is underutilized in young people with mood disorders that do not respond to drug treatment and psychotherapy. A careful analysis of the ethical issues in deciding on the use of ECT in adolescence finds no ethical reason to preclude its use in this age group (Cohen et al., 2000b). They note the inherent conflict between respect for the patient's autonomy and the principle of beneficence. The special dilemma of high vulnerability calls forth overprotection in a desire not to do harm and unrealistic fears regarding the side effects of ECT. Cautiousness recommends the use of ECT in limited indications of catatonia, mood disorders, and intractable acute psychotic disorders. These authors examined the long-term effects on cognition (Cohen et al., 2000) and on the attitudes of both patients and their parents (Taieb et al., 2001) finding no support for the overcautiousness that limits the use of ECT in this age group.

Prejudice against ECT in Patients with Mental Retardation

The presence of mental retardation does not protect patients from serious psychiatric disorders. Yet, when psychosis, depression, or mania is superimposed, treatments are delayed or limited by concerns that medications, and surely ECT, as unsafe for the underlying disability (Thuppal & Fink, 1999; Little et al., 2002). Complicating the application of ECT are difficulties in assuring the diagnosis in patients who may not comprehend or cooperate in the examination, concerns about the effects of induced seizures on compromised brain function, and issues of consent. The latter are a special concern that appears to be insurmountable without recourse to court proceedings. Yet, the reports of the benefits of ECT in patients who were severely incapacitated with mental retardation argue that a more permissive approach to the use of ECT is warranted. An example of the useful treatment of a patient with severe mental retardation is described.

ECT IN MENTAL RETARDATION

A 23-year-old woman with a life-long history of mental retardation was admitted to a psychiatric service with clinical signs of catatonia (posturing, mutism, rigidity), refusal to eat requiring special nursing care and occasional tube feedings, incontinence, alternating with uncontrollable screaming and rages requiring restraint. Her speech was unintelligible to everyone but her mother. This admission was her fifth hospital admission in four years.

Her development and maturation were slow, and the diagnosis of congenital mental retardation was made at an early age. When she was 12, she exhibited temper tantrums that were associated with somnolence. An EEG showed paroxysmal activity and the anticonvulsant carbamazepine (Tegretol) was prescribed. A psychological evaluation showed her intelligence test score at 50. By the time she was sixteen, her tantrums, aggressivity, and periodic uncontrollable excitement warranted another EEG, which was not abnormal. Her behavior worsened, and lithium therapy brought some calming effect. At age 19, she was hospitalized for the first time after four months of depressed mood, failure to eat, and weight loss. Antidepressant and neuroleptic medications were added to the continued treatment with lithium and anticonvulsants. She developed severe dystonia, and all medications were discontinued.

She was hospitalized on four occasions for two to five weeks each, and was treated with different medications. Although ECT was considered a reasonable course of treatment, and with the approval of her parents, no electrotherapist was willing to administer it for lack of proper consent and for concern over the effects of seizures on her brain and behavior.

> Re-examination for epilepsy failed to find evidence, although the EEG
> showed abnormalities that were defined as secondary to the mélange of med-
> ications that were being administered. A diagnosis was made of depressive
> disorder with periodic mania and catatonia in a patient with a mental handi-
> cap. A trial of lorazepam was begun. Although the catatonic behavior did
> diminish, her mood symptoms, periodic excitement, and incontinence
> remained as before.
>
> A course of ECT was begun after both parents signed consent. After two
> bilateral ECT the patient's mood and sleep improved, her appetite returned,
> she was tractable, and she responded to questions and directions. After the
> third treatment, catatonia was gone, and her behavior was well controlled.
> She was discharged to her parents' home for continuation lorazepam and
> weekly ECT.
>
> After two additional treatments, a holiday intervened, she missed a sched-
> uled treatment, and she relapsed into excitement, impulsivity, and
> incontinence. Two treatments the following week restored her behavior. Week-
> ly ECT sustained her life at home, taking part in a day-treatment program for
> patients with a mental handicap. She required no additional medications.
> After four months of treatments, spacing was increased and after nine months,
> further ECT was no longer required.
>
> (Fink, 1999)

The syndrome of behavior outbursts, depression, mania, and catatonia in a
patient with a mental handicap did not differ from the syndrome recognized
as mixed bipolar disorder in those without handicaps. Psychotropic and
anticonvulsant medications served the patient well for a time, but her sensitivity to them precluded their continued use. ECT relieved her acute
syndrome of catatonia and depression, allowed her to remain at home.

Numerous other examples attesting to the safety and efficacy of ECT in
patients with mental retardation are to be found in the literature (Bebchuk et
al., 1996; Van Waarde et al., 2001; Friedlander & Solomon, 2002). The prejudice against the use of ECT in this population and concerns about the proper
application of consent further disadvantage this population of severely ill.

Prejudices against ECT among Chronic Mentally Ill

ECT may be effective in many chronic psychiatric illnesses. Yet, few of the
hospitals dedicated to the care of these severe psychiatrically ill provide facilities for ECT. It is common practice for patients to be maintained on complex
medication cocktails for months, years, and even decades without a trial of

ECT. The failure of state services to provide care is well documented in the reports from California and Texas, where only one state hospital in each state has the facility for ECT. In New York, this deficiency is recognized in a Second Chance program that has been designed to avail long-stay patients of the facilities in an academic institution with panoply of psychiatric services (including ECT). Very few patients, however, are accommodated in this select program.

An example is culled from the experience at an academic hospital in New York to which patients requiring ECT were sent from a local state facility.

ECT IN CHRONIC MENTAL ILLNESS

A 44-year-old woman had been hospitalized since age 24 for a manic illness. From the outset, she had been abusive, aggressive to fellow patients and staff, cursed and spit when interrupted during hours of repetitive circling about the ward, touching walls and chairs. Periodically, she became grossly psychotic, screaming and biting staff members, undressing and throwing her clothes about. She mumbled phrases repetitively, and was often in physical restraint or in an isolation room. Some relief was afforded by large doses of anti-psychotic drugs administered orally and by injection.

When she was first admitted to the state facility, she had improved with a course of ECT and was able to return to the community. In two successive hospitalizations, ECT was useful, but after her admission seven years earlier, ECT was no longer available and the treatment was not offered.

She was seen by a consultant who agreed to admit her to an academic hospital for the purpose of administering ECT. Consent was asked of the patient and refused. A guardian was appointed and an application to the court resulted in approval for a course of ECT. She was transferred to the academic unit with 24-hour nursing care and restriction to an isolation room. ECT was begun under ketamine and succinylcholine anesthesia, and after three treatments, she no longer was aggressive or screaming. She was moved to a standard room and required attendants only during the day. After six ECT, she was pleasant, cooperative, guarded, self-isolating, and speaking only occasionally. She allowed showering and washing her hair. In the third week, she attended group activities and showed interest in the games played by other patients, still speaking little. After 12 ECT, she was outgoing and cooperative and her attendants were discharged. She walked about the unit, attending to her meals, disturbing no one.

She was returned to the state hospital for aftercare. Continuation ECT was offered and discharge planning begun. Relatives had long abandoned her, and she was transferred to a community residence. Over the next few years, she decompensated periodically, requiring re-admission to the academic hospital for ECT, to which she voluntarily consented.

(Fink)

In the centuries before modern bacteriology found ways to treat the infectious diseases associated with mental disorders (such as syphilis and tuberculosis), admission to a state hospital was feared, for it meant that the patient would rarely be discharged. For a few decades in the 20th century, when the somatic treatments were introduced, optimism returned and admission to a state hospital was not regarded as a life long sentence (Braslow, 1997). The drive for deinstitutionalization and the subsequent failure to provide adequate community care is once again associated with low remission rates and high likelihood of inadequate care, chronicity of illness, and homelessness.

Exceptional Position of Criminals with Superimposed Psychiatric Illness

The inadequacy of psychiatric care is further emphasized among psychiatric patients incarcerated after breaking the law. The care in the special hospitals for criminals with superimposed psychiatric illness is even more restricted than in other state facilities. As a consequence, physical and chemical restraints and isolation chambers are the main options available to control unruly prisoners. ECT may be an effective treatment for the excitement and aggression of psychiatric patients as illustrated in an extreme example.

ECT IN CRIMINALLY INSANE

A 27-year old man was imprisoned for murder. In time, he exhibited episodic manic episodes, and on one occasion, severely harmed a guard. Thereafter, he was maintained in solitary confinement. A public defender noted the signs of mania and asked for a psychiatric consultation. The diagnosis of bipolar disorder with psychosis was made and medications prescribed. These muted the prisoner's behavior but whenever he was taken from solitary confinement, his behavior became uncontrolled. A course of ECT was prescribed but the prisoner was deemed incompetent to consent. The public defender presented the dilemma to a judge who called for independent consultations to advise him as to the likelihood of success with ECT. Two consultants from outside the State were called and with hesitation, the judge approved a limited number of treatments.

For each treatment, the patient was transferred from the prison facility under heavy guard, fully shackled, and in restraints. After six treatments, the patient's demeanor changed and it seemed reasonable to allow him into the general prison. Follow-up treatments were not provided, and within two months, his behavior was again severely manic and he was again placed in solitude. The prisoner, recognizing the benefits of the treatment, requested ECT. Since he was considered incompetent by virtue of his prisoner status as well as his illness, permission once again had to be obtained from the court. A limited number of treatments were approved, and the patient again responded. This time, continuation treatments were also approved and the prisoner was enabled to continue his imprisonment under less restricted conditions.

(Fink)

The evidence for the efficacy of ECT in the management of manic excitement is strong. In the situation in which ECT is considered as a special treatment with restricted rules, its benefits can only be obtained by prisoners with the permission of a court. Such impediments to proper care deprive prisoners of the opportunity for treatments that are beneficial.

Summary

Equal opportunity for medical care for all citizens is widely judged as a right. The rule asks that special consideration be shown for biologically and socially disadvantaged persons in order to mitigate their disadvantages. Psychiatrically ill persons belong to disadvantaged groups that have a right to the best available treatment and care. The limited availability of an effective and safe treatment as ECT among psychiatric treatment facilities does not comply with the United Nations Declaration of Human Rights or with the Principles of Policy in Mental Health adopted by the General Assembly.

It is also against the Declaration and the Principles for Policy in Mental Health that ECT is used in a discriminatory fashion. Broad ethnic and underprivileged groups do not have access to the treatment in some countries. The restricted availability of ECT among adolescents, the elderly and the chronically mentally ill, as well as mentally retarded and criminals with superimposed psychiatric illness is an unacceptable discrimination.

It is thought-provoking that the decision-making of a medical treatment is transferred from experts in psychiatry to nonexpert courts.

Denying ECT an appropriate place among psychiatric treatments and not making it available on equal conditions for all people who need it does not comply with the ethical principle of justice.

CHAPTER 8

Balancing Ethical Principles

The practice of ECT should comply with basic ethical principles. Such an ideal is possible in practices that aim at evidenced-based care. The patient referred for ECT has typically had one or several previous depressive episodes and has responded poorly to psychotherapy and medicines, the latter even after lengthy well-monitored trials and at high doses. He has agreed to receive ECT and may even have asked for it. Memory disturbances occur during the treatment but soon vanish as previously impaired social functions are regained. The principle of justice is respected when all psychiatric treatment centers are equipped to provide it for those in need and when all patients at the same treatment facility have equal access to the treatment.

The consideration of ECT is limited by difficulties in the consent process. It is necessary to describe the treatment for the patient and family members, and to repeat the description again at the time of signing the consent. When a good patient-doctor relationship has been established, consent is most often obtained. Misconceptions can be corrected, especially when the patient is given the opportunity to ask questions. Fellow patients who have been treated with ECT may contribute to the information. By the fact that they have recovered from a severe psychiatric illness, they may advocate the treatment.

When the complexity of the treatment and the clinical condition of the patient makes compliance with all the principles difficult, it is necessary to set priorities among them.

Beneficence versus Nonmaleficence

The following vignette illustrates a complex choice between the principles to do good and not to cause harm.

BENEFICENCE VERSUS NONMALEFICENCE

A 70-year-old widow is admitted for the fourth episode of melancholic depression. She is severely agitated, anxious, and restless, neither sitting nor lying down for more than a short time. She repeatedly accuses herself of not having been obedient to her parents in her childhood. Her first two depressive episodes occurred before the age of 50, and each remitted with drug treatment. In a third episode five years ago, she did not respond to medications and was successfully treated with ECT. The present episode of agitated depression is of three months duration, without response to clomipramine and haloperidol.

Two years earlier, she suffered a cerebral thrombosis in a right cerebral artery and was left with a residual weakness in her left arm and leg and evidence of persistent cerebral damage. She has compromised cardiac functions. Her blood pressure is considered hypertensive (190/120 mm Hg) and she has left cardiac enlargement. After moderate exercise, she becomes breathless and her ankles are swollen at the end of the day. The retinal arteries are tortuous but she has no papillary edema.

She is suffering from a psychotic episode in a recurrent depression. ECT is judged to be the treatment of choice but since it is associated with elevation in blood pressure, it may entail risks. Simultaneously, her agitation may be contributing to the elevated blood pressure and exerting a strain on the impaired cardiovascular functions. After consultation with a cardiologist, it was decided to offer ECT with the expectation that relief of the mental disorder may have a beneficial effect on the blood pressure as well as her mental illness.

After eight ECT which were accomplished without complication, the patient was free of symptoms. The blood pressure stabilized at 160/100 mm Hg. A beta-receptor blocking drug and continuation clomipramine were prescribed as a stabilizing regime.

(Ottosson)

The treatment choice is either to pursue an inefficient medication course or to change to ECT. The anticipated consequences of continued drug treatment are prolonged, possibly chronic, illness and sustained strain on the cardiovascular system with a risk of new strokes. The ECT alternative implies a hope of rapid remission, as on the previous occasion. The short-term increase in cardiovascular strain during seizures is the principal risk, but in the long-term perspective the strain may be decreased by improvement of the depressive-agitated state. Weighing for and against, the choice was in favor of ECT.

In today's practice, hypertension is not an obstacle to ECT and the condition may even be benefited by the decreased emotional tension. By seeing hypertension not only as a contraindication against but also as an additional indication for ECT, both the depression and the somatic disease can be alleviated.

Beneficence versus Respect for Autonomy: Irrational Refusal of Treatments

Another contest between two principles of ethics is seen in the following instance from consultation-liaison psychiatry.

BENEFICENCE, RESPECT FOR AUTONOMY AND SUBSTITUTED CONSENT

A 35-year-old homemaker is brought to the emergency department of the local hospital with cut wrists from a suicide attempt. A friend, knowing that the patient was alone at home, decided to visit when she was in the vicinity, and found the patient bleeding severely.

The wounds were sutured, a blood transfusion given, and she was transferred to the psychiatric department. She expressed disappointment at failing to take her life, and stated that she was tired of living. She described awakening each morning at 3 a.m., full of anguish and brooding over her existence. When her husband went on a business journey, she decided to put an end to her travail.

On examination, she looked deeply depressed but was not retarded. The husband and the patient denied marital discord. Both expressed longing for a child. A diagnosis of suicidal depression was made. The patient refused all treatment since she wanted to die. As she was deemed competent, her determination had to be respected as long as the she was voluntarily admitted. On the other hand, it would be irresponsible not to offer her a treatment that gave hope of relief. To make it possible to treat her despite her objection, her admission status was converted to compulsory care according to the current mental health act in Sweden. The husband agreed with the action.

Seemingly indifferent she made no resistance when being treated and coercion was not needed. She recovered after four ECT. She was grateful for having been returned to life and relieved of her depression.

Continued discussion disclosed disappointment at not becoming pregnant. Consultation with a gynecologist was arranged.

(Ottosson)

The psychiatrist has either to respect an irrational decision and abstain from all treatment, or to prioritize the principle of beneficence. The first choice entails possible chronic illness with risk of suicide; the second necessitates compulsory care which, although disagreeable to the patient, makes treatment possible. The overriding commitment of doctors to save life resulted in prioritizing treatment. Since compliance with oral medications would probably be poor, a second choice had to be made between ECT and the injection of antidepressant drugs. ECT was preferred because of its record of faster and more secure effects. The appreciation of the patient indicates that an appropriate choice had been made. The disclosure of involuntary childlessness implied a way to alleviate a possible causal factor.

Beneficence versus Respect for Autonomy: Neither Consent nor Refusal

Some patients are indifferent to recommended treatments. At such times, treatment decisions have to be made by the doctors.

NEITHER CONSENT NOR REFUSAL

A 40-year-old woman comes to the emergency department at the hospital with her 18-year-old daughter who had initiated the consultation. The daughter relates that her mother, usually extroverted, active, and easy-going, has undertaken no initiatives, avoided company, and sighed heavily for the previous month. She awakens early each morning and wanders about restlessly. She accuses herself of being a bad mother and says that such persons as she should not be allowed to live. Her daughter gives a very favorable opinion that the childhood was full of tenderness and stimulation. The reason for going to the hospital was that a farewell letter had been found, ending: "Now I cannot go on any longer. Forgive me."

The patient is silent while her daughter talks. She only states that the daughter must tell everything that she had done. When asked if she accepts being admitted to the department of psychiatry, the patient replies, after a long latency, that nothing matters.

During the following days, her behavior is unchanged. She seems to understand that she is depressed and in need of treatment. Since the depression is a psychotic form, ECT is judged to be the most effective treatment. When it is offered, the patient again answers that nothing matters. The following two days the psychiatrists discuss the treatment and get the same answer.

Since the patient neither consents nor refuses treatment, coercion is not needed and conversion to compulsory care is not made. The patient does not offer resistance when prepared for ECT. After two treatments, her retardation has diminished and after six treatments she is her usual self according to the daughter. On her return home, the patient expresses gratitude for her care.

(Ottosson)

The patient's behavior was an example of depressive indecisiveness. Her illness called for treatment. Since she lacked the capacity to make decisions, a paternalistic attitude was ethically defensible. The choice was between treatment with a prospect of rapid success and nursing care with a protracted wait for a spontaneous remission. To relieve suffering and prevent suicide, the application of antidepressant treatment was prioritized. The alternatives to ECT were antidepressant drugs alone, or combined with neuroleptic drugs. Such treatments are less efficient, slower in action, and have more side effects than ECT. Poor compliance with drug treatment was also a consideration in the decision.

Irrational Consent to ECT

Is it ethical to accept an irrational consent? Consider the following vignette.

IRRATIONAL CONSENT

A 35-year-old civil servant has been admitted to a general hospital after a suicide attempt by a self-inflicted gunshot wound to the chest. The bullet barely missed the heart and the big vessels. After surgical repair and a short stay at the surgical department, the patient was transferred for psychiatric care.

The patient deeply regretted that his suicide had failed. He accused himself of having caused his family undue suffering and complained that he had caused difficulties at work. He reported self-accusatory voices that verified his low opinion of himself. His wife reported that his demeanor had changed during the last few weeks. He had become withdrawn. During the previous two autumns, he had experienced periods of overactivity and expansiveness. He had started a firm to exploit a revolutionary invention that had failed, incurring debts for his family.

A diagnosis of psychotic depressive episode in a bipolar disorder was made. In view of the risk of suicide, ECT was offered. Without hesitation, he consented saying that he "was to die anyhow."

(Ottosson)

According to the accepted criteria, this patient was competent but gave an irrational reason to consent to ECT. Although the acceptance of such consent for an appropriate treatment may be questionable from an ethical point of view, the urgency to relieve depression and the principle of beneficence was prioritized. The alternative, to wait for a spontaneous remission or for the patient to become sufficiently aware of his illness to give informed consent, risked suicidal actions. A paternalistic attitude was in the best interest of the patient. After his recovery, he was offered lithium prophylaxis.

Beneficence versus Family Refusal

The following case vignette brings up the question whether family members may overrule medical decisions.

BENEFICENCE VERSUS FAMILY REFUSAL

A 36-year-old man was admitted to a psychiatric hospital with the diagnosis of catatonia. He had an eight-year history of psychiatric symptoms with psychotic, depressive, and obsessive-compulsive features. Catatonic symptoms became more evident, consisting of posturing, such as hunching over in his seat and standing in one place until he was led to a chair. He exhibited grimacing, automatic obedience, waxy flexibility, echopraxia, and transient periods of mutism. Intermittent refusal of food which necessitated spoon feeding, medication refusal, and self-neglect were other negativistic behaviors. He was treated with a combination of neuroleptic, antidepressant, and sedative medications, and as time went on, these were administered by injection. He was only slightly improved. ECT was suggested but his father and brother declined guardianship responsibility to permit the administration of ECT. They feared ECT as too radical and aggressive, unhelpful, and even harmful. Even if helpful, they feared that forced treatment would ruin their relationship with the patient. They were willing to accept a minor improvement as adequate, accepting relief from a catatonic state in which the patient required spoon feeding to the point where he could sit alone in his apartment each day and eat dinner nightly with his father. The psychiatrists concluded that the patient's disability served to draw this close-knit family together.

The more effective treatment was not given.

(Taylor)

The family's unwillingness to assent deprived the patient of a treatment that would likely have been successful. They objected to ECT for fear that it could be harmful but also as an abrogation of a controlling family pattern.

Apart from the question whether ECT would have been successful in this patient, the crucial matter is who should make the medical care decision. While the treatment team's recommendation was based on the ethical principle of beneficence, the family placed higher value on the principle of nonmaleficence. Even if mutual understanding is desirable, we consider that doctors' commitments are to their patients and not to other people or societal institutions, including the family of adult patients. In that regard, there is no reason why ECT should hold an exceptional position among medical treatments. If a patient is in compulsory care, the doctor should make decisions that serve the patient's interest. Interference by families in medical decisions concerning adult relatives would have absurd consequences.

Beneficence versus Justice: Unequal Availability

A conflict between the principles of beneficence and justice arises often. A tragic experience is reported from an academic medical center in which ECT was not available, Patients who required ECT at that center had to be transferred to a private hospital.

BENEFICENCE VERSUS JUSTICE

A 35-year-old single woman was admitted to the hospital emergency room. She had been running, naked and screaming, down city streets. On admission, she was calm for some moments and then became agitated, warranting physical restraint and injections of lorazepam and haloperidol. Soon after admission, she ran down the hall, tore off her gown, and tried to grab a trauma patient. She provided minimal history, but said she had not been able to sleep for three days, unable to go to work or eat, crying much of the time. For thirteen years she had been employed in one position and had no history of a previous psychiatric illness.

The patient was uncooperative, agitated, and often screaming. She could not be directed. On the second day, she attempted to tear down the door to her room, fracturing two fingers. She responded calmly, but her behavior and consciousness fluctuated wildly. She appeared depressed, occasionally answered questions, and denied suicidal ideation, hallucinations, or disordered thoughts. At times, she spoke loudly to God, insisting that he answer her. Her behavior fluctuated from stupor and mutism to overactivity and agitation, requiring physical and chemical restraint, the latter including haloperidol to 60 mg/day and lorazepam to 12 mg/day.

A diagnosis of manic delirium was made and neurological consultation requested. Lumbar puncture, CSF examination, CT scan, MRI, and EEG displayed normal conditions. On the eighth day she was transferred to the neurology service for further work-up. Lumbar punctures were repeated and found to be bloody. She was treated with intravenous antibiotics for presumed viral encephalitis.

By the second week, she refused to answer questions, staring and posturing with waxy positions of her hands in the air and arching of the back and head, turning to the left. She was alert with a blank stare and her behavior was waxing and waning.

To sedate her for EEG, MRI, and lumbar puncture, she was given intravenous lorazepam (2mg) on three occasions. Within 10 minutes of each injection, she was alert, cooperative, and friendly, asking where she was and what was being done. After one such session, she spoke calmly to her brother and on another occasion to her mother and friends. Within an hour, however, she relapsed to her stuporous state.

Psychiatric consults recommended ECT as the treatment for the catatonic state. The neurologists and internists, however, saw her as too ill for this treatment, refusing 'to clear' her for ECT. For three weeks, she became progressively less alert, requiring parenteral feeding and total nursing care. During one such gastric feeding, on the 45th hospital day, the gastric tube was badly placed, and an aspiration pneumonia and death ensued.

(Fink & Taylor, 2003)

The psychiatrist recommended the appropriate treatment but the medical staff was untutored in ECT and assumed that its risks were far greater than waiting for a spontaneous resolution. It was also an administrative burden that had she been permitted to get ECT, she would have had to be transferred to another institution. The formal principle of justice that persons with the same illness are to be treated equally was not respected.

Beneficence versus Justice: Legal Restrictions

A particularly sad instance is the travail of Andrea Yates, a mother who killed her children during a psychotic illness. She was declared competent to stand trial and was convicted and imprisoned (Christian, 2002a-c; Krauthammer, 2002; Reuters, 2002; Yardley 2002a-c; O'Malley, 2004).

BENEFICENCE VERSUS JUSTICE: LEGAL RESTRICTION ON ECT

Mrs. Yates, a 37-year-old woman in Texas, developed a psychotic illness soon after the birth of her first child in 1994. After the birth of her fourth child in 1999, she again became depressed, despondent, mute, withdrawn, and incapable of caring for her children. At the end of 2000, she delivered her fifth child. She was guilt-ridden and delusional. Twice she attempted suicide. Treatment with the antipsychotic haloperidol improved her condition so that she was considered capable of caring for her children. In March, 2001 her depression worsened and she expressed guilt over the death of her father. She was hospitalized, ECT was considered but rejected. She was again treated with haloperidol but her delusions persisted. She was allowed to return home despite the persistence of her illness.

In May, 2001 she serially drowned and killed her five children, called her husband at his work and urged him to come home immediately as the children had come to harm. He returned to find the children dead.

In the prison hospital, Mrs. Yates described visions of men, children, and horses on the jail walls. She had killed her children because they were "not righteous," were "doomed to perish in the fires of hell," and "to save them from Satan." She was placed on suicidal precautions and for a month she was mute, unresponsive, staring, and posturing.

She was indicted for murder in a jury trial. During the court testimony, a psychiatric expert for the offense argued that it was ". . . reasonable to assume Yates killed the children because of her psychotic delusions. She was massively depressed and withdrawn, nearly mute, and might have benefited greatly from electric shock treatment." The court found her guilty of murder and not to be insane, and ordered her to be imprisoned for life.

(Christian, 2002a, b, and c)

Mrs. Yates was suffering from a psychotic depression, an illness that is remarkably responsive to ECT and poorly responsive to medications. A 1993 Texas law, however, severely restricted the use of ECT, prohibited its use in children under age 16, and prescribed specific regulations that forced its use as a last resort after all other treatment options had failed. These restrictions are onerous, so much so that the treatment is available in only one of the state's psychiatric hospitals, and in only a handful of private and university hospital centers. ECT was considered by her physicians, but the law had so burdened its application that it was unavailable to her.

As if the deaths of her children had not been tragic enough, the imprisonment for life of this clearly psychotic woman is inhumane. We cannot reach another conclusion than the unavailability of ECT for Mrs. Yates makes the Texas legislature, Governor, and the courts complicit in the deaths of her children.

Texas is not unique in this regard. Many hospitals that treat the psychiatrically ill do not provide ECT for their patients, nor do they educate their clinicians in its use. In denying ECT, patients are forced to alternatives with lesser efficacy and greater risk.

Beneficence versus Justice: Legal Interference

Legal interference with judicial complicity in the application of ECT is widespread, mainly by the complex rules for consent (often consent for each treatment, not only for a course of treatments), injunctions that ECT be considered as the last resort, and the onerous demands for reporting of each treatment to an official public agency. An almost paradoxical example of legal interference with medical decisions comes from California.

BENEFICENCE VERSUS JUSTICE: LEGAL INTERFERENCE

A 22-year-old woman with no previous psychiatric history was admitted to a California psychiatric service ten days after a cesarean section. Shortly after delivery she became fearful, acted bizarrely, and had a personality change accompanied by delusional thinking. She believed that she was "psychic," able to read people's minds. She exhibited severe mood swings, displayed little interest in caring for her newborn child, and had difficulty concentrating her thoughts. On the urging of her family, the patient admitted herself voluntarily to the psychiatric service.

On admission, she was floridly psychotic and had a slightly raised temperature. She was diagnosed with an affective disorder, and treatment with lithium carbonate and perphenazine was begun. Three days after admission, she became agitated, more labile and delusional and no longer cooperated with care. The dose of perphenazine was increased, lorazepam was added to the regimen, and almost continuous physical restraints were needed. She required individual nursing care.

To continue treatment, the law required that a judicial hearing be held to determine if the severity of her clinical state permitted the patient to be held against her will. While awaiting the hearing, treatment was continued with court approval. Immediately after the first hearing, a second hearing was convened to determine if the patient could be treated involuntarily with medicine. The judge denied permission to administer medication involuntarily and ordered that the patient be given medication only when she wanted it. Systematic treatment with psychotropic medication was stopped.

Intravenous fluids and physical restraints were required to maintain hydration. The patient lost weight. Increasingly agitated, she was given fluphenazine hydrochloride, which was administered only when she accepted it. By the tenth day she had a creatine kinase level of 876 units per liter- indicating renal failure—and a pulse rate of 120 beats per minute. She responded poorly to antipsychotic medication. Concern over the development of a neuroleptic malignant syndrome led to the discontinuation of psychotropic drugs. The neurologist, however, found no evidence of neuroleptic malignant syndrome and medicines were again prescribed.

With no one able to make treatment decisions regarding her health, a petition was prepared requesting the county to appoint a temporary conservator. She continued to express delusions, threatened to harm others, and was increasingly aggressive. Drug treatment gave little clinical change. The creatine kinase level rose to 1,339 units per liter. Symptoms of waxy flexibility, excessive posturing, and negativism developed. All medication was stopped again. After a ten-day delay, an appointed conservator gave permission to do a brain scan. The patient's agitation required nitrous oxide anesthesia for the scan. The attorney objected to the procedure because he considered it to be invasive. He appealed to the county mental health director to overrule the district attorney and block the procedure, demanding that the case be sent to court so that a superior court judge could decide whether the patient would undergo the procedure. It took four days to obtain a court hearing. With no clinical evidence presented to support the objections to the procedure, the judge gave permission to proceed. The scan revealed no pertinent information.

On the 24th day, a decision was made to proceed with electroconvulsive treatment. Under California law, this is permitted in a non-voluntary patient only after all other possible treatment has been tried. The patient's waxy flexibility continued, now accompanied by a scissors-like crossing of the legs and fingers associated with expressed auditory and visual hallucinations. The diagnosis of lethal catatonia was made. As mandated by law, the treating psychiatrist obtained three psychiatric consultants, adding another two days of delay. Each consultant filled out the necessary affidavits, and permission was requested of the conservator. A fifth psychiatrist, appointed by the county, was now required to review the first four opinions, and this added another day of delay.

The case was again referred to the superior court judge for permission to proceed. The court advised that it would take ten days for a hearing. The physicians were concerned that the patient was dying. Consequently, a letter was hand-delivered to the court explaining the urgency. Even so, intervention by the hospital attorney was necessary to speed the legal timetable, and a hearing was held on the patient's 32nd day of hospital stay. With no clinical evidence to the contrary, the judge ruled in favor of the requested treatment. Next day ECT was started.

Within 36 hours, the patient no longer required nasogastric feedings, intravenous fluids, or restraints. Special nursing care was stopped. The patient was sociable and began to feed herself voluntarily. An uneventful course of electroconvulsive treatment followed, and the patient was discharged as recovered.

(Bach-Y-Rita & De Ranieri, 1992)

The judicial procedures posed a serious obstacle in the care for this woman with a lethal psychiatric illness. Although intended to protect the patient's civil rights, the net effect was just the opposite. Without the judicial obstacles that resulted in notable delays, she could have been treated effectively in two weeks, sparing weeks of additional involuntary detention, restraint, and the hazard of the loss of her life. Physicians have obligations to care and cure but are denied the power to make clinical decisions. Instead, this power is left to crowded courts.

Principles of Ethics in Education of Health Care Professionals

Many students in the health care professions feel a disinclination for ECT, a subject about which they have heard unfavorable rumors but lack clinical experience. Others may take a negative standpoint for ideological reasons. In time, some learn from experience, while others persist in their negative thoughts. To minimize the opportunity that the work of psychiatric teams suffers from dissension, discussions from a platform of ethical principles may be profitable. Such questions can be posed:

> Is the primary aim of health care to alleviate suffering in the patients or to make individual health care professionals feel more comfortable?
> Should the principle of beneficence be sacrificed for the sake of personal ideology?
> Should respect for autonomy always have an overriding priority?
> Should obstruction to the formal principle of justice—that equals should be treated equally—be tolerated on a ward, in a catchment area, or in a country?

An analysis in the terms of basic ethical principles offers possibilities of resolving antagonism.

Ethics Casebook

Ethical deliberations about psychoanalytic practice are featured in an ethics case book published by the American Psychoanalytic Association (Dewald and Clark, 2001). It is a model for medical specialists who deal with clinical situations with conflicting interests, such as the care of a severe psychiatric illness that compromises competence and rationality. Regular ethical analyses from a consequentialist perspective will encourage a more consistent handling and greater professional satisfaction with the use of ECT.

Summary

In balancing the principles of ethics, one against another, consideration is given to the consequences of the alternatives. Such analyses may be made intuitively and without using ethical terms, but consistent handling will be accounted for by the explicit ethical argument in the patient record.

Because the primary medical obligation is to preserve life, physicians may override respect for autonomy with incompetent patients as well as with competent patients who give irrational reasons for refusing ECT. Coercion is rarely necessary but is ethically defensible should a patient's life be endangered. Treatment decisions are matters between the patient and the doctor, and courts and families should not be called upon to intercede with decisions on medical treatments, either of medications or ECT. Ethical analysis in health care facilitates compliance with basic medical principles of ethics.

CHAPTER 9
Conclusions

It is often maintained, and rightly so, that every medical measure be applied on the best possible evidence. This attitude does not preclude that health care also has an ethical base. Ethics and evidence of efficacy and safety are complementary aspects in the provision of humane health care.

Ethics may be defined as the systematic reflection on the values that assure that medical actions are beneficent (doing good), nonmaleficent (not doing harm), appreciate autonomy (respect for the individual), and are just (being fair). To assess whether ECT complies with these principles we have used a consequentialist theory of ethics, an analysis that bases its conclusions on the results of alternative actions. Since each principle is binding unless overridden by a competing principle, they are best considered in turn. Only after individual consideration of each principle can priorities be set.

Beneficence

ECT is an effective treatment, indeed the most effective treatment, for some well-defined psychiatric illnesses. As psychiatric illnesses are associated with high mortality, especially from suicide, ECT may be lifesaving. Withholding ECT may jeopardize life. Attempted suicide may be the first sign of a psychiatric illness and completed suicide may be both the first and the last sign. Severe depressive mood disorder, especially the psychotic variety, is the major indication for ECT. Psychotic depression most often presents with delusions—unreasonable self-reproach for insufficient effort, culpable neglect, sinfulness, breakdown of physical health, or economic bankruptcy. Thoughts of death and suicide prevail, leading to unpredictable and fatal actions. Antidepressants drugs and psychotherapy are the usual treatments, but when these are ineffective or partially so, more effective treatments must be considered. To reduce suffering, much is to be gained by offering ECT at an early

123

stage, preferably as a primary treatment in psychotic or suicidal depression. ECT is the most cost-effective option for such conditions.

ECT also has an unrivaled effect in severe mania, lethal catatonia and the neuroleptic malignant syndrome, acute delirious states, and the schizoaffective, cycloid, and postpartum psychoses. Even in some neurological disorders, such as Parkinson's disease, ECT may be effective when standard treatments fail. While these indications make up a smaller set of applications than for severe depressive disorder, the merit of ECT must be considered as having a decisive impact on their course and outcome.

Nonmaleficence

Every medical treatment starts from its first elementary formulations with unknown hazards. With experience, the treatment progresses to more sophisticated, more effective, and less riskful practices. Later formulations achieve greater benefit with lesser side-effects and risks. ECT has such a history, and modern ECT has the right to be judged for its present methods and not to be burdened with the limitations and bad effects that marked the days of exploration.

ECT is a lenient treatment despite what many believe. Although often used in physically frail and medically ill patients, the mortality rate is less than that of minor surgical operations. ECT is preceded by a thorough physical examination with consultation of appropriate specialists. An anesthesiologist participates in the treatment. Modern practice has maximized the benefits and materially reduced the hazards of the treatments.

Studies of brain structure and function have not shown any adverse effects, arguing for a forceful revision of early assumptions of brain damage. Far from causing loss of brain cells, recent animal experiments and clinical observations suggest that seizures stimulate the formation of new neuronal cells and counteracts the breakdown that may occur in severe psychiatric illness. The effect is dose-dependent, that is, it augments with the number of treatments.

We would have liked to be able to assert that ECT has no side effects, but although memory disturbances are commonplace they are rarely severe and even more rarely do they persist. Since mentally ill patients not treated with ECT also complain of memory difficulties, not all the blame can be assigned to ECT.

ECT that has resulted in improvement or in recovery is associated with improvement of learning, parallel with increased attention, concentration, and motivation. Retention is simultaneously impaired, implying a shorter persistence of memory than usual. Subjectively, memory is experienced as improved since patients judge learning more correctly than they judge retention. The duration of impaired retention has varied from less than a week to a few months. It is possible to minimize the time by modifying seizure induction methods.

Patients who complain of long lasting or persistent memory disturbance may or may not have an objective impairment. Perception of subjective memory impairment may be due to persisting depression, old age or dementia, or several previous episodes of depression, irrespective of how they were treated. Most people experience the transient memory disturbance as negligible compared to freedom from the distress of their psychiatric illness.

Despite these realities in the data of ECT studies, the widespread perception is of a risk of severe memory loss that interferes with successful living. It is codified in legislation restricting the use of ECT and contributes to the lack of training of psychiatrists and the failure of practitioners to follow optimized guidelines for practice. The prejudice continues to be reinforced by national commissions set to assess ECT.

Respect for Autonomy

ECT deserves to be regarded as a treatment option in the same manner as any other medical treatment. All medical care, including the medications for mental illnesses, requires the patient's consent. Yet, ECT is particularly burdened by special regulations that inhibit its use and prevent its proper application. Depending on the attitudes in the community and in the psychiatric department, patients may be encouraged or discouraged to accept ECT. Patients need be given enough information and explanations until they understand the benefits and risks of ECT and alternative treatments and are ready to decide.

As competent patients have the right that their decisions are to be respected, incompetent patients and competent patients who make irrational decisions also have a right to the best available treatment. At times, the ethical principle of beneficence may conflict with respect for autonomy, and a choice must be made. In view of the potential gains from an effective treatment, beneficence is to be prioritized when the illness, if left untreated, may lead to long-lasting disability or premature death. In less severe cases, patient refusals are respected and alternative treatments offered. We agree with an attitude of weak paternalism—asking that physicians act as good parents in instances when patients cannot decide for themselves.

We do not endorse coercion. We recognize that with repeated discussion and the friendly response to questions, many patients consent to ECT even when they are psychotic. If they do not consent, however, and the risk for life is severe, coercion may be justified. In practice, coercion occurs rarely and mostly for only the first few treatments. Recovering patients are often able to consent for the completion of a treatment course. When they have recovered, many patients express gratitude for the paternalistic conduct of their psychiatrist. Paternalism is different from authoritarianism, an attitude that reflects insensitiveness and disrespect for patient autonomy and integrity.

Justice

Access to ECT is grossly unequal for psychiatric populations. The inequality has many roots, among which are ignorance, public and professional prejudice, political, legal, and administrative interference, and a lack of parity in insurance coverage of psychiatric and somatic illnesses. Uneven accessibility and limited knowledge of ECT are features among nations and within nations. It is difficult to imagine that the same lack of equality would be allowed to exist in other illnesses that call for rapid treatment, such as coronary artery infarction, acute surgical conditions, or bacterial infections.

State regulations delay and discourage effective treatment. Deleterious effects on the patients' psychological, social, and financial well-being result from regulatory and legislative pressures to protect patients' rights. Ironically, patients suffer as a direct result of concerns for their rights. To paraphrase a title of an old film, "patients may die with their rights on." Substantial discomfort is also caused for the treating physician, staff, and other patients.

The principle of justice is widely not respected.

Where Do We Stand?

Based on the evidence derived from randomized controlled trials and an extensive clinical experience of more than seventy years, convulsive therapy (ECT) is presently the most effective treatment for certain psychiatric illnesses. In consideration of what can be achieved, the mostly transient memory disturbance is a moderate price. The benefit-to-risk ratio of ECT is unusually favorable.

Respect for patient autonomy is the maxim of ECT. Only when a severe psychiatric illness restricts and distorts the decision-making capacity and the consequences of no treatment are serious, is the principle of beneficence given priority over respect for autonomy.

In most cases the use of ECT is in agreement with the principles of beneficence, nonmaleficence, and respect for autonomy. Sadly, the principle of justice is far from satisfied. In democratic countries this means violation of the constitution and the UN Declaration of Human Rights that human beings are equal in dignity and rights.

While we anticipate that ECT will be replaced by an effective and less prejudicial and circumstantial treatment in time, it is an effective and safe treatment that is available today. An urgent goal of mental health care should be to provide access to ECT and eliminate the severe impediments to its use, so long as it can defend an evidence-based superiority over other treatments.

References

Abrams, R. (Ed.). (1989). ECT in the high-risk patient. *Convulsive Therapy, 6,* 1–122.

Abrams, R. (2000). Electroconvulsive therapy requires higher dosage levels. Food and Drug Administration action is required. *Archives of General Psychiatry, 57,* 445–446.

Abrams, R. (2002a). *Electroconvulsive Therapy* (4th ed.). New York: Oxford University Press.

Abrams, R. (2002b). Stimulus titration and ECT dosing. *The Journal of ECT, 18 (1),* 3–9.

Abrams, R., & Essman, W. B. (Eds.). (1982). *Electroconvulsive therapy. Biological foundations and clinical applications.* New York: Spectrum.

Abrams, R., & Fink, M. (1972). Clinical experience with multiple electroconvulsive treatments. *Comprehensive Psychiatry, 13,* 115–121.

Abrams, R., Fink, M., Dornbush, R. L., Feldstein, S., Volavka, J., & Roubicek, J. (1972). Unilateral and bilateral ECT, effects on depression, memory, and electroencephalogram. *Archives of General Psychiatry, 27,* 88–91.

Agence d'Evaluation des Technologies et des Modes d'Intervention en Santé (AETMIS). (2002). The use of electroconvulsive Therapy in Québec. Report prepared by Reiner Banken. Montreal: AETMIS, xvii–96. www.aetmis.gouv.qc.ca.

Als-Nielsen, B., Chen, W., Gluud, C., & Kjaergard, L. L. (2003). Association of funding and conclusions in randomized drug trials: a reflection of treatment effect or adverse events? *Journal of the American Medical Association, 290,* 921–928.

American Psychiatric Association. (1978). *Electroconvulsive therapy.* Task force report #14. Washington, DC: American Psychiatric Association.

American Psychiatric Association. (1990). *The practice of electroconvulsive therapy. Recommendations for treatment, training and privileging.* Washington, DC: APA Press.

American Psychiatric Association. (1993). Practice guidelines for major depressive disorder in adults. *American Journal of Psychiatry, 150,* (Suppl.).

American Psychiatric Association. (2000). Practice guideline for the treatment of patients with major depressive disorder (Rev. ed.). *American Journal of Psychiatry, 157,* (4 Suppl.), 1–26.

American Psychiatric Association. (2001). *The practice of electroconvulsive therapy. Recommendations for treatment, training, and privileging* (2nd ed.). Washington, D.C.: APA Press.

American Psychiatric Association. (2003). A vision for the mental health system from http://www.psych.org/news_room/press_releases/visionreport040303.pdf

Andersen, K., Balldin, J., Gottfries, C-. G., Granerus, A. K., Modigh, K., Svennerholm, L., & Wallin, A. (1987). A double-blind evaluation of electroconvulsive therapy in Parkinson's disease with "on-off" phenomena. *Acta Neurologica Scandinavica, 76,* 191–199.

Andrade, C., Shah, N., & Tharyan, P. (2003). The dilemma of unmodified ECT. *Journal of Clinical Psychiatry, 64:* 1147–1152.

Andersson, J. E., & Bolwig, T. G. (2002). Electroconvulsive therapy in Denmark 1999. A nation-wide questionnaire study [Danish]. *Ugeskrift for Laeger, 164,* 3449–3452.

Anonymous. (1994). How I owe my life to ECT—By a practicing psychiatrist. *The American Journal of Social Psychiatry, 4,* 16–17.

A practicing psychiatrist. (1965). The experience of electro-convulsive therapy. *The British Journal of Psychiatry, 111,* 365–367.

Arnold, O. H., & Stepan, H. (1952). Untersuchungen zur Frage der akuten tödlichen Katatonie. *Wiener Zschr Nervenheilkunde Grenzgebiete, 4,* 235–258.

Avery, D., & Lubrano, A. (1979). DeCarolis study reconsidered. *The American Journal of Psychiatry, 136,* 559–562.

Bach-Y-Rita, G., & De Ranieri, A. (1992). Medicolegal complications of postpartum catatonia. *Western Journal of Medicine, 156,* 417–419.

Basaglia, F. (1968). *Istituzione negata.* Torino: Einaudi.

Basaglia, F., Lovell, A. & Scheper-Hughes, L. (1987). *Psychiatry inside-out. Selected writings of Franco Basaglia.* New York: Columbia University Press.

Beauchamp, T. L., & Childress, J. F. (2001). *Principles of biomedical ethics* (5th ed.). Oxford: Oxford University Press.

Beauchamp, T. L., & Walters, L. R. (Eds.). (1989). *Contemporary issues in bioethics* (3rd ed.). Belmont, CA: Wadsworth Publishing Company.

Bebchuk, J. M., Barnhill, J. & Dawkins, K. (1996). ECT and mental retardation. *American Journal of Psychiatry, 153,* 1231.

Beckmann, H., & Franzek, E. (2000). The genetic heterogeneity of "schizophrenia." *The World Journal of Biological Psychiatry, 1,* 35–41.

Benadhira, R., & Teles, A. (2001). Current status of electroconvulsive therapy in adult psychiatric care in France [French]. *Encephale, 27,* 129–136.

Beresford, H. R. (1971). Legal issues relating to electroconvulsive therapy. *Archives of General Psychiatry, 25,* 100–102

Berger. L., & Vuckovic, A. (1994). *Under observation. Life inside a psychiatric hospital.* New York: Ticknor & Fields. 79–130.

Bergsholm, P., Larsen, J. L., Rosendaahl, K., & Holsten, F. (1989). Electroconvulsive therapy and cerebral computed tomography. *Acta Neurologica Scandinavica, 80,* 566–572.

Berrios, G., & Porter, R. (1995). *A history of clinical psychiatry: The origin and history of psychiatric disorders.* London: Athlone Press.

Birkenhäger, T. K., Pluijms, E. M., & Lucius, S. A. P. (2003). ECT response in delusional versus nondelusional depressed inpatients. *Journal of Affective Disorders, 74,* 191–195.

Blachly, P., & Gowing, D. (1966). Multiple monitored electroconvulsive treatment. *Comprehensive Psychiatry, 7,* 100–109.

Blomquist, C. (1977). From the Oath of Hippocrates to the Declaration of Hawaii. Introductory essay to a draft of an international code of ethics for psychiatrists prepared for the World Psychiatric Association and the CIBA Foundation meeting on the ethical aspects of psychiatry, London, June 1976. *Ethics in Science & Medicine, 4,* 139–149.

Bolwig, T. G., Hertz, M. M., & Vestergaard, E. (1977). Acute hypertension causing blood-brain barrier break-down during epileptic seizures. *Acta Neurologica Scandinavica, 56,* 335–342.

Bond, E. D. (1954a). Results of treatment in psychoses—with a control series. II. Involutional psychotic reaction. *American Journal of Psychiatry, 110,* 881–883.

Bond, E. D., & Morris, H. H. (1954b). Results of treatment in psychoses. III. Manic-depressive reactions. *American Journal of Psychiatry, 110,* 883–885.

Bond, T. C. (1980). Recognition of acute delirious mania. *Archives of General Psychiatry, 37,* 553–554.

Bonds, C., Frye, M. A., Coudreau, M. F., Cunningham, M., Spearing, M., McGuire, M., & Guze, B. (1998). Cost reduction with maintenance ECT in refractory bipolar disorder. *Journal of ECT, 14,* 36–41.

Bostwick, J. M., & Chozinski, J. P. (2002). Temporal competency in catatonia. *The Journal of the American Academy of Psychiatry and the Law, 30,* 371–376.

Bostwick, J. M., & Pankratz, V. S. (2000). Affective disorders and suicide risk. A re-examination. *American Journal of Psychiatry, 157,* 1925–1932.

Brandon, S., Cowley, P., McDonald, C., Neville, P., Palmer, R., & Wellstood-Eason, S. (1984). Electroconvulsive therapy. Results in depressive illness from the Leicester trial. *British Medical Journal, 288,* 22–25.

Braslow, J. (1997). *Mental ills and bodily cures: Psychiatric treatment in the first half of the twentieth century.* Berkeley, CA: University California Press.

Breakey, W. R., & Dunn, G. (in press). Racial disparity in the use of ECT for affective disorders. *American Journal of Psychiatry.*

Breggin, P. R. (1979). *Electro-shock: Its brain-disabling effects.* New York: Springer Publishing Co.

Breggin, P. (1991). *Toxic psychiatry. Why therapy, empathy, and love must replace the drugs, electroshock, and biochemical theories of the "New Psychiatry."* New York: St. Martin's Press.

Bremner, J. D., Narayon, M., Anderson, E. R., Staib, L. H., Miller, H. L., & Charney, D. S. (2000). Hippocampal volume reduction in major depression. *American Journal of Psychiatry, 157,* 115–118.

Briska, W. (1997). *The history of Elgin Mental Health Center. Evolution of a state hospital.* Carpentersville, IL: Crossroads Communications.

Brodersen, P., Paulson, O. B., & Bolwig, T. G. (1973). Cerebral hyperemia in electrically induced epileptic seizures. *Archives of Neurology, 28,* 334–338.

Brookes, G., Rigby, J., & Barnes, R. (2000). Implementing the Royal College of Psychiatrists' guidelines for the practice of electroconvulsive therapy. *Psychiatric Bulletin, 24,* 329–330.

Bush, G., Fink, M., Petrides, G., Dowling, F., & Frances, A. (1996a). Catatonia, I. Rating scale and standardized examination. *Acta Psychiatrica Scandinavica, 93,* 129–136.

Bush, G., Fink, M., Petrides, G., Dowling, F., & Frances, A. (1996b). Catatonia, II. Treatment with lorazepam and electroconvulsive therapy. *Acta Psychiatrica Scandinavica, 93,* 137–143.

Calev, A. (1994). Neuropsychology and ECT. Past and future research trends. *Psychopharmacology Review, 30,* 461–469.

Calev, A., Ben-Tzvi, E., Shapira, B., Drexler H., Carasso R., & Lerer B. (1989). Distinct memory impairments following electroconvulsive therapy and imipramine. *Psychological Medicine, 19,* 111–119.

Calev, A., Gaudino, E. A., Squires, N. K., Zervas, I. M., & Fink, M. (1995). ECT and non-memory cognition. A review. *British Journal of Clinical Psychology, 34,* 505–515.

Calev, A., Korin, Y., Shapira, B., Kugelmass, S., & Lerer, B. (1986). Verbal and nonverbal recall by depressed and euthymic affective patients. *Psychological Medicine, 16,* 789–794.

Calev, A., Nigal, D., Shapira, B., Tubi, N., Chazan, S., Ben-Yehuda, Y., Kugelmass, S., & Lerer, B. (1991). Early and long-term effects of electroconvulsive therapy and depression on memory and other cognitive functions. *The Journal of Nervous and Mental Disease, 179,* 526–533.

Capron, A. M. (1999). Ethical and human-rights issues in research on mental disorders that may affect decision-making capacity. *New England Journal of Medicine, 340,* 1430–1434.

Carney, S., & Geddes, J. (2003). Electroconvulsive therapy: Recent recommendations are likely to improve standards and uniformity of use [editorial]. *British Medical Journal, 326,* 1343–1344.

Carney, M. W. P., Roth, M., & Garside, R. F. (1965). The diagnosis of depressive syndromes and the prediction of ECT response. *British Journal of Psychiatry, 111,* 659–674.

Castillo, E., Rubin, R. T., & Holsboer-Trachsler, E. (1989). Clinical differentiation between lethal catatonia and neuroleptic malignant syndrome. *American Journal of Psychiatry, 146,* 324–328.

Chanpattana, W., Chakrabhand, S., Kongsakon, R., Techakasem, P., & Buppanharun, W. (1999). The short-term effect of combined ECT and neuroleptic therapy in therapy-resistant schizophrenia. *The Journal of ECT, 15,* 129–139.

Charney, D. (1999). The National Bioethics Advisory Commission report: The response of the psychiatric research community is critical to restoring public trust. *Archives of General Psychiatry, 56,* 699–700.

Childress, J. F., & Shapiro, H. T. (1999). Almost persuaded. Reactions to Oldham et al. *Archives of General Psychiatry, 56,* 697–698.

Christian, C. (2002a, March 6). Yates was in 'severe' state of psychosis. *Houston Chronicle.*

Christian, C. (2002b, March 8). Key to Yates' defense disputed. *Houston Chronicle.*

Christian, C. (2002c, March 8). Expert witness can't say whether Yates was legally insane. *Houston Chronicle.*

Chung, K-.F., Cheung, H. K. (2003). Electroconvulsive therapy in Hong Kong. *Psychiatric Bulletin, 27,* 102–104.

Church of Scientology. (1998). *What is Scientology?* Los Angeles: Bridge Publications.

Coffey, C. E., Weiner, R. D., Djang, W. T., Figiel, G. S, Soady, S. A. R., Patterson, L. J., Holt, P. D., Spritzer, C. E., & Wilkinson, W. E. (1991). Brain anatomic effects of electroconvulsive therapy: A prospective magnetic resonance imaging study. *Archives of General Psychiatry, 48*, 1013–1021.

Cohen, D., Flament, M., Taieb, O., Thompson, C., & Basquin, M. (2000a). Electroconvulsive therapy in adolescence. *European Child & Adolescent Psychiatry, 9*, 1–6.

Cohen, D., Flament, M., Dubos, P. F., & Basquin, M. (1999). Case series, catatonic syndrome in young people. *Journal of the American Academy of Child and Adolescent Psychiatry, 38*, 1040–1046.

Cohen, D., Taieb, O., Flament, M., Benoit, N., Chevret, S., Corcos, M., Fossati, P., Jeannet, P., Allilaire, J. F., & Basquin, M. (2000b). Absence of cognitive impairment at long-term follow-up in adolescents treated with ECT for severe mood disorder. *American Journal of Psychiatry, 157*, 460–462.

Cole, C., & Tobiansky, R. (2003). Electronconvulsive therapy. NICE guidance may deny patients' treatment that they may benefit from. *British Medical Journal, 327*, 621.

Consensus Conference. (1985). Electronconvulsive therapy. *Journal of the American Medical Assocation, 254*, 103–108.

Coryell, W., & Winokur G. (1992). Course and outcome. In E. S. Paykel (Ed.). *Handbook of Affective Disorders* (2nd ed., pp. 89–108). Edinburgh U.K.: Churchill Livingstone.

Crismon, M. L., Trivedi, M. H., Pigott, T. A., Rush, A. J., Hirschfeld, R. M. A., Kahn, D. A., DeBattista, C., Nelson, J. C., Nierenberg, A. A., Sackeim, H. A., & Thase, M. E. (1999). The Texas medication algorithm project. Report of the Texas consensus conference panel on medication treatment of major depressive disorder. *The Journal of Clinical Psychiatry, 60*, 142–156.

Cronholm, B., & Ottosson, J.-O. (1961). Memory functions in endrogenous depression. Before and after electroconvulsive therapy. *Archives of General Psychiatry 5*, 193–199.

Cronholm, B., & Ottosson, J.-O. (1963). The experience of memory function after electroconvulsive therapy. *The British Journal of Psychiatry, 109*, 251–258.

Culver, C. M., Ferrell, R. B., & Green, R. M. (1980). ECT and special problems of informed consent. *The American Journal of Psychiatry, 137*, 586–591.

Dam, A. M., & Dam, M. (1986). Quantitative neuropathology in electrically induced general convulsions. *Convulsive Therapy, 2*, 77–89.

DeCarolis, V., Gilbert, F., Roccatagliata, G., et al. (1964). Imipramina ed elettroshock nella terapia delle depressioni, analysi clinico-statistica dei resultati in 437 casi. *Sistema Nervoso, 1*, 29–42.

D'Elia, G., & Raotma, H. (1975). Is unilateral ECT less effective than bilateral ECT? *The British Journal of Psychiatry, 126*, 83–89.

D'Elia, G., & Raotma, H. (1977). Memory impairment after convulsive therapy: Influence of age and number of treatments. *Archiv fur Psychiatrie und Nervenkrankheiten, 223*, 219–226.

Deutsch, A. (1937/1946). *The mentally ill in America. A history of their care and treatment from colonial times.* New York: Columbia University Press.

Devanand, D. P., Verma, A. K., Tirumalasetti, F., & Sackeim, H. A. (1991). Absence of cognitive impairment after more than 100 lifetime ECT treatments. *The American Journal of Psychiatry, 148,* 929–932.

Dewald, P. A., & Clark, R. W. (2001). *Ethics case book of the American Psychoanalytic Association.* New York: The American Psychoanalytic Association.

DiMascio, A., & Shader, R. I. (1972). *Butyrophenones in psychiatry.* New York: Raven Press.

Donahue, A. B. (2000). Electroconvulsive therapy and memory loss: A personal journey. *The Journal of ECT, 16,* 133–143.

Douyon, R., Serby, M., Klutchko, B., & Rotrosen, J. (1989). ECT and Parkinson's disease revisited, a "naturalistic" study. *The American Journal of Psychiatry, 146,* 1451–1455.

Duffett, R., & Lelliott, P. (1998). Auditing electroconvulsive therapy: The third cycle. *The British Journal of Psychiatry, 172,* 401–405.

Editor. (1981). ECT in Britain: A shameful state of affairs. *The Lancet, 1,* 1207–1208.

Editor. (1983). Impaired autonomy and rejection of treatment. *Journal of Medical Ethics, 9,* 131–132.

Ende, G., Braus, D. F., Walter, S., Weber-Fahr, W., & Henn, F. A. (2000). The hippocampus in patients treated with electroconvulsive therapy, a proton magnetic resonance spectroscopic imaging study. *Archives of General Psychiatry, 57,* 937–943.

Endler, N. S. (1982). *Holiday of darkness: A psychologist's personal journey out of his depression.* New York: John Wiley & Sons.

Endler, N. S., & Persad, E. (1988). *Electroconvulsive therapy, the myths and the realities.* Toronto, Canada: Hans Huber Publishers.

Eranti, S. V., & McLoughlin, D. M. (2003). Electroconvulsive therapy—State of the art. *The British Journal of Psychiatry, 182,* 8–9.

Eriksson K. I., & Westrin C. G. (1995). Coercive measures in psychiatric care: Reports and reactions of patients and other people involved. *Acta Psychiatrica Scandinavica, 92,* 225–230.

Evans, J. P. M., Graham-Smith, D. G., Green, A. R., & Tordhoff, A. F. C. (1976). Electroconvulsive shock increases the behavioural responses of rats to brain 5-hydroxytryptamine accumulation and central nervous system stimulant drugs. *British Journal of Pharmacology, 6,* 193–199.

Evans, R., Naik, P. C., & Alikhan, S. (2003). Conflicting advice confuses prescribers. *British Medical Journal, 327,* 621.

Exner, J. E., Jr., & Murillo, L. G. (1973). Effectiveness of regressive ECT with process schizophrenia. *Diseases of the Nervous System, 34,* 44–48.

Fairweather, D. B., Ashford, J., & Hindmarch, I. (1996). Effects of fluvoxamine and dothiepin on psychomotor abilities in healthy volunteers. *Pharmacology, Biochemistry, and Behavior, 53,* 265–269.

Fink, M. Cholinergic aspects of convulsive therapy. *The Journal of Nervous and Mental Disease, 142,* 475–484.

Fink, M. (1979). *Convulsive therapy, theory and practice.* New York: Raven Press.

Fink, M. (1990). How does convulsive therapy work? *Neuropsychopharmacology, 3,* 73–82.

Fink, M. (1991). Impact of the anti-psychiatry movement on the revival of ECT in the U.S. *The Psychiatric Clinics of North America, 14,* 793–801.

Fink, M. (1996). Neuroleptic malignant syndrome and catatonia. One entity or two? *Biological Psychiatry, 39,* 1–4.

Fink, M. (1997). Prejudice against electroshock. Competition with psychological philosophies as a contribution to stigma. *Convulsive Therapy,* 13, 253–265.

Fink, M. (1998). ECT and clozapine in schizophrenia. *The Journal of ECT, 14,* 223–226.

Fink, M. (1999a). *Electroshock, Restoring the Mind.* New York, Oxford University Press. Reissued in paperback *Electroshock, Healing Mental Illness,* 2002.

Fink, M. (1999b). Delirious mania. *Bipolar Disorders, 1,* 54–60.

Fink, M. (2000). Electroshock revisited. *American Scientist, 88 (2),* 162–167.

Fink, M. (2002). Move on! Commentary on R. Abrams, stimulus titration and ECT dosing. *The Journal of ECT, 18,* 11–12.

Fink, M. (2003). A beautiful mind and insulin coma: Social constraints on psychiatric diagnosis and treatment. *Harvard Review of Psychiatry,* 11, 1–7.

Fink, M., Abrams, R., Bailine, S., & Jaffe, R. (1996). Ambulatory electroconvulsive therapy: Task force report of the Association for Convulsive Therapy. *Convulsive Therapy,* 12, 42–55.

Fink, M., Bailine, S., & Petrides, G. (2001). Electrode placement and electroconvulsive therapy, a search for the chimera. *Archives of General Psychiatry, 58,* 607–608.

Fink, M., & Kahn, R. L. (1957). Relation of EEG delta activity to behavioral response in electroshock. Quantitative serial studies. *Archives of Neurology and Psychiatry 1957, 78,* 516–525.

Fink, M., & Klein, D. F. (1995). An ethical dilemma in child psychiatry. *Psychiatric Bulletin, 19,* 650–651.

Fink M., & Ottosson J.-O. (1980). A theory of convulsive therapy in endogenous depression. Significance of hypothalamic functions. *Psychiatry Research, 2,* 49–61.

Fink, M., & Sackeim, H. A. (1996). Convulsive therapy in schizophrenia. *Schizophrenia Bulletin, 22(1),* 27–39.

Fink, M., & Taylor, M. A. (2003) *Catatonia: A clinician's guide to diagnosis and treatment.* Cambridge UK: Cambridge University Press.

Fishbein, I. L. (1949). Involutional melancholia and convulsive therapy. *The American Journal of Psychiatry, 106,* 128–135.

Fochtmann, L. K. J. (1994). Animal studies of electroconvulsive therapy. Foundations for future research. *Psychopharmacology Bulletin, 30,* 321–444.

Folkerts, H. (1996). The ictal encephalogram as a marker for the efficacy of electroconvulsive therapy. *European Archives of Psychiatry and Clinical Neuroscience, 246,* 155–164.

Foucault, M. (1965). *Madness and civilization. A history of insanity in the age of reason.* New York: Pantheon Books.

Frame, J. (1984). *An angel at my table: Autobiography 2.* London: Falmingo (Harper Collins).

Frank, L. R. (1978). *The history of shock treatment.* San Francisco: Leonard Frank.

Frankel, F. H. (1977). Current perspectives on ECT, A discussion. *The American Journal of Psychiatry, 134,* 1014–1119.

Frankenburg, F. R., Suppes, T., & McLean, P. E. (1993). Combined clozapine and electroconvulsive therapy. *Convulsive Therapy, 9,* 176–80.

Fraser, M. (1982). *ECT: A clinical guide.* New York: John Wiley & Sons.

Freeman, C. P. L., Basson, J. V., & Crighton, A. (1978). Double-blind controlled trial of electroconvulsive therapy (E.C.T) and simulated E.C.T in depressive illness. *Lancet, 1,* 738–740.

Freeman, C. P. L., Hendry, J., & Fergusson, G. (2000). National audit of electroconvulsive therapy (ECT) in Scotland. www.sean.org.uk/report/report00.htm.

Freeman, H. (1986). *Judge, jury and executioner.* Urbana, IL: Talking Leaves Publishing Co.

Freeman, W., Watts, J. W., & Hunt, T. (1942). *Psychosurgery: Intelligence, emotion and social behavior following prefrontal lobotomy for mental disorders.* Springfield IL: Charles C. Thomas.

Fricchione, G. L., Kaufman, L. D., Gruber, B. L., & Fink, M. (1990). Electroconvulsive therapy and cyclophosphamide in combination for severe neuropsychiatric lupus with catatonia. *The American Journal of Medicine, 88,* 443–444.

Friedberg, J. (1976). *Shock treatment is not good for your brain.* San Francisco, CA: Glide Publications.

Friedberg, J. (1977). Shock treatment, brain damage, and memory loss. A neurological perspective. *The American Journal of Psychiatry, 134,* 1010–1014.

Friedel, R. O. (1986). The combined use of neuroleptics and ECT in drug resistant schizophrenic patients. *Psychopharmacology Bulletin, 22,* 928–930.

Friedlander, R. I., & Solomon, K. (2002). ECT: Use in individuals with mental retardation. *Journal of ECT, 18,* 38–42.

Gabbard, K., & Gabbard, G. O. (1999). *Psychiatry and the cinema.* Chicago: University of Chicago Press.

Gagne, G. G., Furman, M. J., Carpenter, L. L., & Price, L. H. (2000). Efficacy of continuation ECT and antidepressant drugs compared to long-term antidepressants alone in depressed patients. *The American Journal of Psychiatry, 157,* 1960–1965.

Gangadhar, B. N., Kapur, R. L., & Kalyanasundaram, S. (1982). Comparison of electroconvulsive therapy with imipramine in endogenous depression, a double blind study. *The British Journal of Psychiatry, 141,* 367–371.

George, M. S., & Belmaker R. H. (2000). *Transcranial magnetic stimulation in neuropsychiatry.* Washington DC: American Psychiatric Press.

Glassman, A. H., Kantor, S. J., & Shostak, M. (1975). Depression, delusions, and drug response. *The American Journal of Psychiatry, 132,* 716–719.

Glen, T., & Scott, A. I. F. (2000). Variation in rates of electroconvulsive therapy use among consultant treatment teams in Edinburgh (1993–1996). *Journal of Affective Disorders, 58,* 75–78.

Gotkin, J., & Gotkin, P. (1975). *Too much anger, too many tears.* New York: Quadrangle Books.

Graham, P. J., & Foreman, D. M. (1995). An ethical dilemma in child and adolescent psychiatry. *Psychiatric Bulletin, 19,* 84–86.

Grahame-Smith, D. G., Green, A. R., & Costain, D. W. (1978). Mechanism of antidepressant action of electroconvulsive therapy. *Lancet, 1,* 254–257.

Gray, E. G., (1983). Severe depression, a patient's thoughts. *The British Journal of Psychiatry, 143,* 319–322.

Greenberg, L. B., Gage, J., Vitkun, S., & Fink, M. (1987). Isoflurane anesthesia therapy: A replacement for ECT in depressive disorders? *Convulsive Therapy, 3,* 269–277.

Greenblatt, M., Grosser, G. H., & Wechsler, H. (1964). Differential response of hospitalized depressed patients to somatic therapy. *The American Journal of Psychiatry, 120,* 935–943.

Gregory, S., Shawcross, C. R., & Gill, D. (1985). The Nottingham ECT study: A double-blind comparison of bilateral, unilateral and simulated ECT in depressive illness. *The British Journal of Psychiatry, 146,* 520–524.

Grisso, T., & Appelbaum, P. (1998). *MacArthur competence assessment tool for treatment (MacCAT-T).* Sarasota, FL: Professional Resource Press.

Grob, G. N. (1994). *The mad among us: A history of the care of America's mentally ill.* New York: The Free Press.

Group for the Advancement of Psychiatry. (1947, September 15), *Shock therapy* [letter, see Fink (1979), p. 14].

Grunhaus, L. J., Barroso, L. W. (1989). *Electroconvulsive therapy, the treatment, the questions, the answers.* Lake Oswego, OR: MECTA Corporation.

Grunhaus, L., Pande, A. C., & Haskett, R. F. (1990). Full and abbreviated courses of maintenance electroconvulsive therapy. *Convulsive Therapy, 6,* 130–138.

Gujavarty, K., Greenberg, L., & Fink, M. (1987). Electroconvulsive therapy and neuroleptic medication in therapy-resistant positive symptom psychosis. *Convulsive Therapy, 3,* 185–195.

Guze, S. B. (1967). The occurrence of psychiatric illness in systemic lupus erythematosus. *The American Journal of Psychiatry, 123,* 1562–1570.

Hale, N. G. (1995). *The rise and crisis of psychoanalysis in the United States: Freud and the Americans, 1917–1985.* New York: Oxford University Press.

Harmer, C. J., Bhagwagar, Z., Cowen, P. J., & Goodwin, G. M. (2002). Acute administration of citalopram facilitates memory consolidation in healthy volunteers. *Psychopharmacology, 163,* 106–110.

Hartelius, H. (1952). Cerebral changes following electrically induced convulsions: An experimental study on cats. *Acta Psychiatrica et Neurologica Scandinavica* (Suppl. 77), 1–128.

Healy, D. (1997). *The anti-depressant era.* Cambridge, MA: Harvard University Press.

Healy, D. (2002). *The creation of psychopharmacology.* Cambridge, MA: Harvard University Press.

Healy, D. (2003). *Let them eat Prozac.* Toronto, Canada: James Lorimer Press.

Healy, D, & Thase, M. E. (2003). Is academic psychiatry for sale? *The British Journal of Psychiatry, 182,* 388–390.

Helmchen, H., & Okasha, A. (2000). From the Hawaii declaration to the Declaration of Madrid. *Acta Psychiatrica Scandinavica* (Suppl. 399), 20–23.

Hermann, R. C., Dorwart, R. A., Hoover, C. W., & Brody, J. (1995). Variation in ECT use in the United States. *The American Journal of Psychiatry, 152,* 869–875.

Hermann, R. C., Ettner, S. L., Dorwart, R. A., Hoover, C. W., & Yeung, E. (1998). Characteristics of psychiatrists who perform ECT. *The American Journal of Psychiatry, 155,* 889–894.

Hermann, R. C., Ettner, S. L., Dorwart, R. A., Langman-Dorwart, N., & Kleinman, S. (1999). Diagnoses of patients treated with ECT, a comparison of evidence-based standards with reported use. *Psychiatric Services, 1999,* 1059–1065.

Hordern, A., Holt, N. F., Burt, C. G., & Gordon, W. F. (1963). Amitriptyline in depressive states, phenomenology and prognostic considerations. *The British Journal of Psychiatry, 109,* 815–825.

Hubbard, R. (1951). *Dianetics: The original thesis.* Wichita, KS: Wichita Publishing Co.

Hubbard, R. (1951). *Science of survival: Prediction of human behaviour.* Sussex, UK: Publications Organization World Wide.

Hunter, R., & Macalpine, I. (1982). *Three hundred years of psychiatry 1535–1860.* Hartsdale, NY: Carlyle Publishing.

Hurford, W. E. (1999). Sedation in the intensive care unit. *International Anesthesiology Clinics, 37,* 113–122.

Huston, P. E., & Locher, L. M. (1948a). Involutional psychosis: Course when untreated and when treated with electric shock. *Archives of Neurology and Psychiatry, 59,* 385–394.

Huston, P.E., & Locher, L.M. (1948b). Manic-depressive psychosis. Course when untreated and when treated with electric shock. *Archives of Neurology and Psychiatry, 60,* 37–48.

Imlah, N. W., Ryan, E., & Harrington, J. A. (1965). The influence of antidepressant drugs on the response to electroconvulsive therapy and on subsequent relapse rates. *Neuropsychopharmacology, 4,* 438–442.

Institute of Medicine, Committee on Quality of Health Care in America. (2001). *Crossing the quality chasm. A new health system for the 21st century.* Washington DC: National Academies Press.

Isaac, R. J., & Armat, V. C. (1990). *Madness in the streets: How psychiatry and the law abandoned the mentally ill.* New York: The Free Press.

Isaac, R. J., & Brakel, S. J. (1992). Subverting good intentions, a brief history of mental health law "reform." *Cornell Journal of Law and Public Policy, 2,* 89–119.

Isometsa, E. T., Henricksson, M. M., Heikkinen, M. E., & Lonnqvist, J. K. (1996). Completed suicide and recent electroconvulsive therapy in Finland. *Convulsive Therapy, 12,* 152–155.

Jacobs, B. L., van Praag, H., & Gage, F. H. (2000). Adult brain neurogenesis and psychiatry. A novel theory of depression. *Molecular Psychiatry, 5,* 263–269.

Janicak, P. G., Davis, J. M., Gibbons, R. D., Ericksen, S., Chang, S., & Gallagher, P. (1985). Efficacy of ECT, a meta-analysis. *The American Journal of Psychiatry, 142,* 297–302.

Janis, I. L. (1950). Psychologic effects of electric convulsive treatments (changes in word association reactions). *The Journal of Nervous and Mental Disease, 111,* 469–489.

Johnson, A. B. (1990). *Out of bedlam. The truth about deinstitutionalization.* New York: Basic Books.

Johnson, S. Y. (1993). Regulatory pressures hamper the effectiveness of electroconvulsive therapy. *Law and Psychology Review, 17,* 155–170.

Johnstone, E. C., Deakin, J. F., Lawler, P., Frith, C. D., Stevens, M., McPherson, K., & Crow, T. J. (1985). The Northwick Park electroconvulsive therapy trial. *Lancet, 2,* 1317–1320.

Kalinowsky, L. B., & Hippius, H. (1969). *Pharmacological, convulsive and other somatic treatments in psychiatry.* New York: Grune & Stratton.

Kalinowsky, L. B., Hippius, H., & Klein, H. E. (1982). *Biological treatments in psychiatry*. New York: Grune & Stratton.

Kantor, S. J., & Glassman, A. H. (1977). Delusional depressions, natural history and response to treatment. *The British Journal of Psychiatry, 131*, 351–356.

Karliner, W., & Wehrheim, H. K. (1965). Maintenance convulsive treatments. *The American Journal of Psychiatry, 121*, 113–115.

Kellner, C. H. (2001). Towards a modal ECT treatment. *The Journal of ECT, 17*, 1–2.

Kellner, C. H., & Fink, M. (2002). The efficacy of ECT and "treatment resistance." *The Journal of ECT, 18*, 1–2.

Kellner, C. H., Fink, M., Knapp, R., Petrides, G., Husain, M., Rummans, T., Mueller, M., Bernstein, H., Rasmussen, K., O'Connor, K., Smith, G., Rush, A. J., Biggs, M., McClintock, S., Bailine, S., & Malur, C. (submitted). Suicide risk and ECT. *The American Journal of Psychiatry*.

Kesey, K. (1972). *One flew over the cuckoo's nest*. New York: Viking Press.

Khan, A., Khan, S., Kolts, R., & Browen, W. A. (2003). Suicide rates in clinical trials of SSRIs, other antidepressants, and placebo: Analysis of FDA reports. *The American Journal of Psychiatry, 160*, 790–792.

Kho, K. H., van Vreeswijk, M. F., Simpson, S., & Zwinderman, A. H. (2003). A meta-analysis of electroconvulsive therapy efficacy in depression. *The Journal of ECT, 19*, 139–147.

Kiloh, L. G. (1961). Pseudo-dementia. *Acta Psychiatrica Scandinavica, 37*, 336–351.

Kiloh, L. G., Smith, J. S., & Johnson, G. F. (1988). *Physical treatments in psychiatry*. Melbourne, Australia: Blackwell Scientific Publications.

King, P. D. (1958). Regressive EST, chlorpromazine, and group therapy in treatment of hospitalized chronic schizophrenics. *The American Journal of Psychiatry, 115*, 354–357.

Klapheke, M. M. (1991a). Clozapine, ECT, and schizoaffective disorder, bipolar type. *Convulsive Therapy, 7*, 36–39.

Klapheke, M. M. (1991b). Follow-up on clozapine and ECT. *Convulsive Therapy, 7*, 303–305.

Klapheke, M. M. (1993). Combining ECT and antipsychotic agents. Benefits and risks. *Convulsive Therapy, 9*, 241–255.

Klerman, G. L. (1990). The psychiatric patient's right to effective treatment. Implications of *Osheroff vs. Chestnut Lodge. The American Journal of Psychiatry, 147*, 409–418.

Kneeland, T. W., & Warren, C. A. B. (2002). *Pushbutton psychiatry: A history of electroshock in America*. Westport, CT & London: Praeger.

Kosel, M., & Schlaepfer, T. E. (2003). Beyond the treatment of epilepsy, new applications of vagus nerve stimulation in psychiatry. *CNS Spectrums, 8*, 515–521.

Koukopoulos, A. (1993). ECT. Why so little in Italy? *International Journal of Psychiatry and Behavioral Sciences, 3*, 79–81.

Kramer, B. A. (1985). Use of ECT in California, 1977–1983. *The American Journal of Psychiatry, 142*, 1190–1192.

Kramer, B. A. (1986). Maintenance ECT. A survey of practice. *Convulsive Therapy, 3*, 260–268.

Kramer, B. A. (1990). Maintenance electroconvulsive therapy in clinical practice. *Convulsive Therapy, 6*, 279–286.

Kramer, B. A. (1999). Use of ECT in California, revisited, 1984–1994. *The Journal of ECT, 15,* 245–251.

Krauthammer, C. (2002, March 15) Not guilty, insane. *Washington Post,* A23.

Kroessler, D. (1985). Relative efficacy rates for therapies of delusional depression. *Convulsive Therapy, 1,* 173–182.

Kronfol, Z., Schlesser, M., & Tsuang, M. T. (1977). Catatonia and systemic lupus erythematosus. *Diseases of the Nervous System, 38,* 729–731.

Krystal, A. D., Dean, M. D., Weiner, R. D., Tramontozzi III, L. A., Connor, K. M., Lindahl, V. H., & Massie, R. W. (2000). ECT stimulus intensity, are present ECT devices too limited? *The American Journal of Psychiatry, 157,* 963–967.

Krystal, A. D., Watt, B. V., Weiner, R. D., Moore, S., Steffens, D. C., & Lindahl, V. (1998). The use of flumazenil in the anxious and benzodiazepine-dependent ECT patient. *The Journal of ECT, 14,* 5–14.

Lambourn, J., & Gill, D. (1978). A controlled comparison of simulated and real ECT. *The British Journal of Psychiatry, 133,* 514–519.

Landy, D. A. (1991). Combined use of clozapine and electroconvulsive therapy. *Convulsive Therapy, 7,* 218–221.

Langer, G., Neumark, J., Koenig, G., Graf, M., & Schonbeck, G. (1985). Rapid psychotherapeutic effects of anesthesia with isoflurane (ES narcotherapy) in treatment-refractory depressed patients. *Neuropsychobiology, 14,* 118–120.

Langer, G., Karazman, R., Neumark, J., Saletu, B., Schonbeck, G., Grunberger, J., Dittrich, R., Petriceck, W., Hoffman, P., Linzmayer, L., Anderer, P., & Steinberger, K. (1995). Isoflurane narcotherapy in depressed patients refractory to conventional antidepressant drug treatment. *Neuropsychobiology, 31,* 182–194.

Lapid, M. I., Rummans, T. A., Poole, K. L., Pancratz, V. S., Maurer, M. S., Rasmussen, K. G., Philbrick, K. L., & Appelbaum, P. S. (2003). Decisional capacity for severely depressed patients requiring electroconvulsive therapy. *The Journal of ECT, 19,* 67–72.

Lask, B., Britten, C., Kroll, L., Magagna, J., & Tranter, M. (1991). Children with pervasive refusal. *Archives of Disease in Childhood, 66,* 866–869.

Latey, R. H., & Fahy, T. J. (1986). *Electroconvulsive therapy in the Republic of Ireland 1982.* Galway, Ireland: Galway University Press.

Lauritzen, L., Odgaard, K., Clemmesen, L., Lunde, M., Öhrström, J., Black, C., & Bech, P. (1996). Relapse prevention by means of paroxetine in ECT-treated patients with major depression, a comparison with imipramine and placebo in medium-term continuation therapy. *Acta Psychiatrica Scandinavica, 94,* 241–251.

Lebensohn, Z. M. (1984). Electroconvulsive therapy. Psychiatry's villain or hero? *The American Journal of Social Psychiatry, 4,* 39–43.

Lesser, H. (1983). Consent, competency and ECT. A philosopher's comment. *Journal of Medical Ethics, 9,* 144–145.

Levkovitz, Y., Caftori, R., Avital, A., & Richter-Levin, G. (2002). The SSRIs drug fluoxetine, but not the noradrenergic tricyclic drug desipramine improves memory performance during acute major depression. *Brain Research Bulletin, 58,* 345–350.

Lisanby, S. H., & Belmaker, R. H. (2000). Animal models of the mechanism of action of repetitive transcranial magnetic stimulation (rTMS). Comparisons with electroconvulsive shock (ECS). *Depression & Anxiety, 12,* 178–187.

Lisanby, S. H., Maddox, J. H., Prudic, J., Devanand, D. P., & Sackeim, H. A. (2000). The effects of electroconvulsive therapy on memory for autobiographical and public events. *Archives of General Psychiatry, 57,* 581–590.

Lisanby, S. H., Schlaepfer, T. E., Fisch, H. U., Sackeim, H. A. (2001) Magnetic seizure therapy of major depression. *Archives of General Psychiatry, 58,* 303–305.

Little, J. D., McFarlande, J., Ducharme, H. M. (2002). ECT use delayed in the presence of comorbid mental retardation. A review of clinical and ethical issues. *The Journal of ECT, 18,* 218–222.

Little, J. D., Ungvari, G. S., & McFarlane, J. (2000). Successful ECT in a case of Leonhard's cycloid psychosis. *The Journal of ECT, 16,* 62–67.

Mac, D. S., & Pardo, M. P. *(1983).* Systemic lupus erythematosus and catatonia. A case report. *Journal of Clinical Psychiatry, 44(4),* 155–156.

MacDonald, R. P. (1984). Medical, ethical and legal considerations of electroconvulsive therapy. *Osgoode Hall Law Journal, 22,* 683–710.

MacQueen, A. R. (2002). Is it ethical to ignore significant mental health problems? *Australian and New Zealand Journal of Psychiatry, 36,* 426–427.

MacQueen, G. M., Galway, T. M., Hay, J., Young, L. T., & Joffe, R. T. (2002). Recollection memory deficits in patient with major depressive disorder predicted by past depressions but not current mood state or treatment status. *Psychological Medicine, 32,* 251–258.

Madsen, T. M., Treschow, A., Bengzon, J., Bolwig, T. G., Lindvall, O., & Tingström, A. (2000a). Increased neurogenesis in a model of electroconvulsive therapy. *Biological Psychiatry, 47,* 1043–1049.

Madsen, T. M., Greisen, M. H., Nielsen, S. M., Bolwig, T. G., & Mikkelsen, J. D. (2000b). Electroconvulsive stimuli enhance both neuropeptide Y receptor Y1 and Y2 messenger RNA expression and levels of binding in the rat hippocampus. *Neuroscience, 98,* 33–39.

Maixner, D. F., & Krain, L., (2003, September). Case report. Lupus, catatonia, and medicolegal complexities. Personal communication.

Malitz, S., & Sackeim, H. (Eds.) (1986). Electroconvulsive therapy. Clinical and basic research issues. *Ann. NY Acad. Science, 462,* 1–424.

Mann, J. J., Malme, K. M., Diehl, D. J., Perel, J., Cooper, J. B., & Mintun, M. A. (1996). Demonstration in vivo of reduced serotonin responsivity in the brain of untreated depressed patients. *The American Journal of Psychiatry, 153,* 174–182.

Manning, M. (1994). *Undercurrents: A therapist's reckoning with depression.* San Francisco: HarperCollins.

Markowitz, J., Brown, R., Sweeney, J., & Mann, J. J. (1987). Reduced length and cost of hospital stay for major depression in patients treated with ECT. *The American Journal of Psychiatry, 144,* 1025–1029.

Marneros, A., Pillmann, F., Haring, A., & Balzuweit, S. (2000). Acute and transient psychotic disorders. *Fortschritte der Neurologie-Psychiatrie, 68* [Suppl. 1], S22–S25.

Martin, B. A., & Bean, G. J. (1992). Competence to consent to electroconvulsive therapy. *Convulsive Therapy, 8,* 92–102.

Matthews, E. (2000). Autonomy and the psychiatric patient. *Applied Philosophy, 17,* 59–70.

McCall, W. V., Reboussin, D. M., Weiner, R. D., & Sackeim, H. A. (2000). Titrated moderately suprathreshold vs fixed high-dose right unilateral electroconvulsive therapy. *Archives of General Psychiatry, 57,* 438–444.

Medical Research Council. (1965). Clinical trial of the treatment of depressive illness. *Lancet, 1,* 881–886.

Meduna, L. (1935). Versuche über die biologische Beeinflussung des Ablaufes der Schizophrenie. I. Campher und Cardiozolkrämpfe. *Z. Neurological Psychiatry, 152,* 235–262.

Meduna, L. (1937). *Die Konvulsionstherapie der Schizophrenie.* Halle, Germany: Carl Marhold.

Mendels, J. (1965). Electroconvulsive therapy and depression. II. Significance of endogenous and reactive syndromes. *The British Journal of Psychiatry, 111,* 682–686.

Mental Health Act Commission. (2001). *Ninth Biennial Report 1999–2001.* London: Stationery Office.

Merskey, H. (1999). Ethical aspects of the physical manipulation of the brain. In S. Bloch, P.Chodoff, & S. Green (Eds.). *Psychiatric ethics* (3rd ed.). Oxford: Oxford University Press.

Michels, R. (1999, May 6). Are research ethics bad for mental health? *The New England Journal of Medicine, 340,* 1427–1430.

Michigan Mental Health Code, Act 258 of 1974. 330.1717, sec. 717.

Miller, F. G., & Fins, J. J. (1999). Protecting vulnerable research subjects without unduly constraining neuropsychiatric research. *Archives of General Psychiatry, 56,* 701–702.

Morgan, R. F. (1985). *Electric shock.* Toronto, Canada: IPI Publishing Ltd.

Moynihan R. (2003). Who pays for the Pizza? Redefining the relationships between doctors and drug companies. 1. Entanglement. *British Medical Journal, 326,* 1189–1192.

Mudur, G. (2002). Indian group seeks ban on the use of electroconvulsive therapy without anaesthesia. *British Medical Journal, 324,* 806.

Mukherjee, S., Sackeim, H. A., & Schnur, D. B. (1994). Electroconvulsive therapy of acute manic episodes. A review of 50 years' experience. *The American Journal of Psychiatry, 151,* 169–176.

Mulsant, B. H., Haskett, R. F., Prudic, J., Thase, M. E., Malone, K. M., Mann, J. J., Pettinati, H. M., & Sackeim, H. A. (1997). Low use of neuroleptic drugs in the treatment of psychotic major depression. *The American Journal of Psychiatry, 154,* 559–561.

Murray, C. J. L., & Lopez, A. D. (Eds). (1996). *Global health Statistics. A compendium of incidence, prevalence and mortality estimates for over 200 conditions.* Boston, MA: Harvard University Press.

Murray, C. J. L., & Lopez, A. D. (1997a). Global mortality, disability, and the contribution of risk factors. Global Burden of Disease Study. *Lancet, 349,* 1498–1504.

Murray, C. J. L., & Lopez, A. D. (1997b). Alternative projections of mortality and disability by cause 1990–2020. Global Burden of Disease Study. *Lancet, 349,* 1436–1442.

National Advisory Mental Health Council (2003, January). Insel T. *National Institute of Mental Health Director's Report.*

National Board of Health and Social Welfare. (1994). *ECT treatment in psychiatry* [In Swedish with English summary]. Stockholm: Socialstyrelsen.

National Commission for the Protection of Human Subjects of Biomedical and Behavioral Research. (1977). *Report and Recommendations.* DHEW Publications (OS) 77–0001. Washington DC: US Government Printing Office, Appendix.

National Responsibility Board. (1996). A disciplinary case [Swedish]. *HSAN* 364/96.

Nobler, M. S., Luber, B., Moeller, J. R., Katzman, G. P., Prudic, J., Devanand, D. P., Dichter, G. S., & Sackeim, H. A. (2000). Quantitative EEG during seizures induced by electroconvulsive therapy. Relations to treatment modality and clinical features. 1. Global analyses. *The Journal of ECT, 16,* 211–228.

Nowakowska, E., Chodera, A., & Kus, K. (1996). Anxiolytic and memory improving activity of fluoxetine. *Polish Journal of Pharmacology, 48,* 255–260.

Nuland, S. B. (2003). *Lost in America. A journey with my father.* New York: Alfred A. Knopf.

O'Connor, M. K., Knapp, R., Husain, M., Rummans, T. A., Petrides, G., Smith, G., Mueller, M., Snyder, K., Bernstein, H., Rush, A. J., Fink, M., & Kellner, C. (2001). The influence of age on the response of patients with major depression to electroconvulsive therapy. *The American Journal of Geriatric Psychiatry, 9,* 382–390.

Okasha, A. (2003). The Declaration of Madrid and its implementation. An update [editorial]. *World Psychiatry, 2,* 65–67.

Okasha, A., & Tewfik, G. I. (1964). Haloperidol—A controlled clinical trial in chronic disturbed psychotic patients. *The British Journal of Psychiatry, 110,* 56–60.

Oldham, J. M., Haimowitz, S., & Delano, S. J. (1999a). Protection of persons with mental disorders from research risk. A response to the report of the National Bioethics Advisory Commission. *Archives of General Psychiatry, 56,* 688–693.

Oldham, J. M., Haimowitz, S., & Delano, S. J. (1999b). Reply. *Archives of General Psychiatry, 56,* 703–704.

Olfson, M., Marcus, S., Sackeim, H. A., Thompson, J., & Pincus, H. A. (1998). Use of ECT for the inpatient treatment of recurrent major depression. *The American Journal of Psychiatry, 155,* 22–29.

O'Malley S. (2004). *Are you there alone?* New York: Simon and Schuster.

Oquendo, M., Kamali, M., Ellis, S., Grunebaum, M., Malone, K., Brodsky, B., Sackeim, H., & Mann, J. (2002). Adequacy of antidepressant treatment after discharge and the occurrence of suicidal acts in major depression. A prospective study. *The American Journal of Psychiatry, 159,* 1796–1751.

Ottosson, J.-O. (1960). Experimental studies of the mode of action of electroconvulsive therapy. *Acta Psychiatrica Scandinavica* (Suppl. 145), 1–141.

Ottosson, J.-O. (1985). Use and misuse of electroconvulsive treatment. *Biological Psychiatry, 20,* 933–946.

Ottosson, J.-O. (1970). Influence of age on memory impairment after electroconvulsive therapy. *Acta Psychiatrica Scandinavica* (Suppl. 219), 154–165.

Ottosson, J.-O. (1986). Clinical perspectives on mechanism of action. In S. Malitz, H. A. Sackeim, (Eds.). *Electroconvulsive Therapy: Clinical and basic research issues. Annals of the New York Academy of Science, 462,* 357–365.

Ottosson, J.-O. (1991). Is unilateral nondominant ECT as efficient as bilateral ECT? A new look at the evidence. *Convulsive Therapy, 7,* 190–200.

Ottosson, J.-O. (1992). Ethics of electroconvulsive therapy. *Convulsive Therapy, 8,* 233–236.

Ottosson, J.-O. (1995). Ethical aspects of research and practice of ECT. *Convulsive Therapy, 11,* 288–299.

Ottosson, J.-O. (2000). The Declaration of Hawaii and Clarence Blomquist. *Acta Psychiatrica Scandinavica, 101* (Suppl. 399), 16–19.

Ottosson, J.-O. (2003). *Psykiatrin i Sverige: Vägval och vägvisare* [Swedish]. Stockholm: Natur och Kultur.

Ottosson, J.-O. (2004). *Psykiatri,* 6th ed. [Swedish]. Stockholm: Liber AB.

Packman, W. L., Cabot, M. G., & Bongar, B. (1994). Malpractice arising from negligent psychotherapy. Ethical, legal, and clinical implications of *Osheroff v. Chestnut Lodge. Ethics and Behavior, 4,* 175–197.

Palmer, R. L. (1981). *Electroconvulsive therapy, an appraisal.* New York: Oxford University Press.

Parker, G., Roy, K., Hadzi-Pavlovic, D., & Pedic, F. (1992). Psychotic (delusional) depression. A meta-analysis of physical treatments. *Journal of Affective Disorders, 24,* 17–24.

Parry, B. L. (1981). The tragedy of legal impediments involved in obtaining ECT for patients unable to give informed consent. *The American Journal of Psychiatry, 138,* 1128–1129.

Pellegrino, E. D. (1998). Emerging ethical issues in palliative care. *JAMA, 279,* 1521–1522.

Peralta, V., & Cuesta, M. J. (2003). Cycloid psychosis. A clinical and nosological study. *Psychological Medicine, 33,* 443–453.

Perris, C. (1974). A study of cycloid psychoses. *Acta Psychiatrica Scandinavica* (Suppl. 253).

Petrides, G., Fink, M., Husain, M. M., Rush, A. J., Knapp, R., Mueller, M., Rummans, T., O'Connor, K., Rasmussen, K., Biggs, M., Bailine, S., & Kellner, C. (2001). ECT remission rates in psychotic versus non-psychotic depressed patients. A report from CORE. *The Journal of ECT, 17,* 244–253.

Pfleiderer, B., Michael, N., Erfurth, A., Ohrmann, P., Hohmann, U., Wolgast, M., Fiebich, M., Arolt, V., & Heindel, W. (2003). Effective electroconvulsive therapy reverses glutamate/glutamine deficit in the left anterior cingulum of unipolar depressed patients. *Psychiatry Research, 122,* 185–192.

Philpot, M., Treloar, A., Gormley, N., & Gustafson, L. (2002). Barriers to the use of electroconvulsive therapy in the elderly. A European survey. *European Psychiatry, 17,* 41–45.

Pillmann, F., Haring, A., Balzuweit, S., Bloink, R., & Marneros, A. (2001). Concordance of acute and transient psychoses and cycloid psychoses. *Psychopathology, 34,* 305–311.

Pippard, J. (1992). Audit of electroconvulsive treatment in two National Health Service regions. *British Journal of Psychiatry, 160,* 621–637.

Pippard, J., & Ellam, L. (1981). *Electroconvulsive treatment in Great Britain, 1980.* London: Gaskell.

Plum, F., Posner, J. B., & Troy, B. (1968). Cerebral metabolic and circulatory responses to induced convulsions in animals. *Archives of Neurology, 18,* 1–13.

Porter, R. (2002). *Madness: A brief history.* New York: Oxford University Press.

Prudic, J., & Sackeim, H. A. (1999). Electroconvulsive therapy and suicide risk. *The Journal of Clinical Psychiatry, 60* (Suppl. 2), 104–110.

Quétel, C. (1990). *History of syphilis.* Translated by J Braddock, & B. Pike. Baltimore, MD: Johns Hopkins Press.

Quill, T. E., Dreser, R., & Brock, D. W. (1997). The rule of double effect—a critique of its role in end-of-life decision making. *New England Journal of Medicine, 337,* 1768–1771.

Rami-Gonzales, L., Bernardo, M., Boget, T., Salamero, M., Gil-Verona, J. A., & Junque, C. (2001). Subtypes of memory dysfunction associated with ECT. Characteristics and neurobiological bases. *The Journal of ECT, 17,* 129–135.

Rasmussen, K. G., & Abrams, R. (1991). Treatment of Parkinson's disease with electroconvulsive therapy. *The Psychiatric Clinics of North America, 14,* 925–933.

Rees, L., & Davies, B. (1965). A study of the value of haloperidol in the management and treatment of schizophrenic and manic patients. *International Journal of Neuropsychiatry, 1,* 263–266.

Reid, W. H., Keller, S., Leatherman, M., & Mason, M. (1998). ECT in Texas. 19 months of mandatory reporting. *The Journal of Clinical Psychiatry, 59,* 8–13.

Reiter-Theil, S. (1992). Autonomy and Beneficence. Ethical issues in electroconvulsive therapy. *Convulsive Therapy, 8,* 237–244.

Relman, A. S., & Angell, M. (2002). America's other drug problem. How the drug industry distorts medicine and politics. *New Republic, 227,* 27–41.

Relton, H. L. (2003). Patients must be confident that evidence of efficacy is compelling. *British Medical Journal, 327,* 621.

Reuters. (2002, March 9). Texas mom insane for two years before crime.

Rey, J. M., & Walter, G. (1997). Half a century of ECT use in young people. *The American Journal of Psychiatry, 154,* 595–602.

Riker, R. R., Fraser, G. L., & Cox, P. M. (1994). Continuous infusion of haloperidol controls agitation in critically ill patients. *Critical Care Medicine, 22,* 433–440.

Roose, S. P., Glassman, A. H., Walsh, B. T., Woodring, S., & Vital-Herne, J. (1983). Depression, delusions, and suicide. *The American Journal of Psychiatry, 140,* 1159–1162.

Rose, D., Wykes, T., Leese, M., Bindman, J., & Fleischman, P. (2003). Patients' perspectives on electroconvulsive therapy. Systematic review. *British Medical Journal, 326,* 1363–1367.

Rosenbach, M. L., Hermann, R. C., & Dorwart, R. A. (1997). Use of electroconvulsive therapy in the Medicare population between 1987 and 1992. *Psychiatric Services, 48,* 1537–1542.

Rosenberg, L. E. (2002). Brainsick. A physician's journey to the brink. *Cerebrum, 4,* 2–10.

Roth, M., & Rosie, J. M. (1953). The use of electroplexy in mental disease with clouding of consciousness. *The Journal of Mental Science, 99,* 103–111.

Roueché B. (1974, Sept. 9) As empty as Eve. *New Yorker,* 84–100.

Royal College of Psychiatrists (1989). *The practical administration of electroconvulsive therapy (ECT).* London: Gaskell.

Royal College of Psychiatrists Special Committee on ECT and the Scottish ECT Audit Network (2003). *Statement on ECT Practice.* http//sean.org.uk/ appraisal. php.

Sackeim, H. A. (Ed.). (1989), *Mechanisms of action. Convulsive Therapy, 6,* 207–310.

Sackeim, H. A. (1991). Are ECT devices underpowered? *Convulsive Therapy, 7,* 233–236.

Sackeim, H. A. (Ed.). (1986). *Electroconvulsive therapy: Clinical and basic research issues.* New York: New York Academy of Sciences.

Sackeim, H. A. (2000). Memory and ECT—From polarization to reconciliation. *The Journal of ECT, 16,* 87–96.

Sackeim, H. A., Luber, B., Katzman, G. P., Moeller, J. R., Prudic, J., Devanand, D. P. & Nobler, M. S. (1996). The effects of electroconvulsive therapy on quantitative electroencephalograms. Relationship to clinical outcome. *Archives of General Psychiatry, 53,* 814–824.

Sackeim, H. A., Prudic, J., Devanand, D. P., Kiersky, J. E. Fitzsimons, L. Moody, B. J. McElhiney, M. C. Coleman, E. A., & Settembrino J. M. (1993). Effects of stimulus intensity and electrode placement on the efficacy and cognitive effects of electroconvulsive therapy. *New England Journal of Medicine, 328,* 839–846.

Sackeim, H. A., Prudic, J., Devanand, D. P., Nobler, M. S., Lisanby, S. H., Peyser, S., Fitzsimons, L., Moody, B. J., & Clark, J. (2000). A prospective, randomised, double-blind comparison of bilateral and right unilateral electroconvulsive therapy at different stimulus intensities. *Archives of General Psychiatry, 57,* 425–434.

Sackeim, H. A., Haskett, R. F., Mulsant, B. H, Thase, M. E., Mann, J. J., Pettinati, H. M., Greenberg, R. M., Crowe, R. R., Cooper, T. B., & Prudic, J. (2001). Continuation pharmacotherapy in the prevention of relapse following electroconvulsive therapy. A randomized controlled trial. *JAMA, 285,* 1299–1307.

Sargant, W., Slater, E., & Dally, P. (1964). *An introduction to physical methods of treatment in psychiatry.* Baltimore, MD: Williams & Wilkins.

Say, R. E., & Thomson, R. (2003). The importance of patient preferences in treatment decisions—challenges for doctors. *British Medical Journal, 327,* 542–545.

Schachter, S. C., & Schmidt, D. (2001). *Vagus Nerve Stimulation.* London: Martin Dunitz.

Schatzberg, A. F. (2003). New approaches to managing psychotic depression. *The Journal of Clinical Psychiatry, 64* (Suppl. 1), 19–23.

Schlaepfer, T. E., Kosel, M., & Nemeroff, C. B. (2003). Efficacy of repetitive transcranial magnetic stimulation (rTMS) in the treatment of affective disorders. *Neuropsychopharmacology, 28,* 201–205.

Schneider, B., Philipp, M., & Muller, M. J. (2001). Psychopathological predictors of suicide in patients with major depression during a 5-year follow-up. *European Psychiatry, 16,* 283–288.

Scottish ECT Audit Network (SEAN). (2002). www.sean.org.uk.

Seager, C. P., & Bird, R. L. (1962). Imipramine with electrical treatment in depression: A controlled trial. *The Journal of Mental Science, 108,* 704–707.

Selected staff. University of Louisville School of Medicine. (1985). 1,250 electroconvulsive treatments without evidence of brain injury. *The British Journal of Psychiatry, 147,* 203–204.

Seneff, M. G., Mathews, R. A. (1995). Use of haloperidol infusions to control delirium in critically ill adults. *Annals of Pharmacotherapy, 29,* 690–693.

Shapira, B., Lerer, B., Kindler, S., Lichtenberg, P., Gropp, C., Cooper, T., & Calev, A. (1992). Enhanced serotonergic responsivity following electroconvulsive therapy in patients with major depression. *The British Journal of Psychiatry, 160,* 223–229.

Sheline, Y. I., Sanghavi, M., Mintun, M. A., & Gado, M. H. (1999). Depression duration but not age predicts hippocampus volume loss in medically healthy women with recurrent major depression. *Journal of Neuroscience, 19,* 5034–5043.

Sherlock, R. (1983). Consent, competency and ECT. Some critical suggestions. *Journal of Medical Ethics, 9,* 141–143.

Shorter, E. (1997). *A history of psychiatry, from the era of the asylum to the age of Prozac.* New York: John Wiley & Sons.

Shuster, E. (1998). The Nuremberg Code, Hippocratic ethics and human rights. *Lancet 351,* 974–977.

Shutts, D. (1982). *Lobotomy. Resort to the knife.* New York: Van Nostrand Reinhold Co.

Small, J. G., Klapper, M. H., Kellams, J. J. Miller, M. J., Milstein, V., Sharpley, P. H., & Small, I. F. (1988). Electroconvulsive treatment compared with lithium in the management of manic states. *Archives of General Psychiatry, 45,* 727–732.

Small, J. G., Small, I. F., Milstein, V., Kellams, J. J., & Klapper, M. H. (1985). Manic symptoms, an indication for bilateral ECT. *Biological Psychiatry, 20,* 125–134.

Somatics, Inc. (1986a). *Informed ECT for health professionals.* Videotape. 24 min. 910 Sherwood Drive, Lake Bluff, IL 60044.

Somatics, Inc. (1986b). *Informed ECT for patients and families.* Videotape. 22 min. 910 Sherwood Drive, Lake Bluff, IL 60044.

Spiessl, H., Hubner-Liebermann, B., & Cording, C. (2002). Suicidal behaviour of psychiatric in-patients. *Acta Psychiatrica Scandinavica, 106,* 134–138.

Squire, L. R., & Chase, P. M. (1975). Memory functions six to nine months after electroconvulsive therapy. *Archives of General Psychiatry 32,* 1557–1564.

Steffens, D. C., Krystal, A. D., Sibert, T. E., Moore, S. D., & Weiner, R. D. (1995). Cost effectiveness of maintenance ECT. *Convulsive Therapy, 11,* 283–284.

Steir, C. (Ed.). (1978). *Blue Jolts.* Washington DC: New Republic Books.

Stone, A. A. (1979). Legal and ethical developments. In L. Bellak (Ed.). *Disorders of the schizophrenic syndrome.* New York, Basic Books, pp. 560–584.

Stone, A. A. (1990). Law, science, and psychiatric malpractice, a response to Klerman's indictment of psychoanalytic psychiatry. *The American Journal of Psychiatry, 147,* 419–427.

Strachan, J. (2001). Electroconvulsive therapy—Attitudes and practice in New Zealand. *Psychiatric Bulletin, 25,* 467–470.

Strömgren, L. S. (1991). Electroconvulsive therapy in the Nordic countries, 1977–1987. *Acta Psychiatrica Scandinavica, 84,* 428–434.

Sutherland, E. M., Oliver, J. E., & Knight, D. R. (1969). EEG, memory and confusion in dominant, non-dominant and bi-temporal ECT. *The British Journal of Psychiatry, 115,* 1059–1064.

Swedish Parliamentary Priorities Commission. Swedish Government Reports SOU 1995: 5. Stockholm: The Ministry of Health and Social Affairs.

Szasz, T. S. (1961). *The myth of mental illness. Foundations of a theory of personal conduct.* New York: Paul B. Hoeber Co.

Szasz, T. S. (1963). *Law, liberty, and psychiatry. An inquiry into social uses of mental health practices.* New York: Macmillan.

Szasz, T. S. (1965). *The ethics of psychoanalysis. The theory and method of autonomous psychotherapy.* New York: Basic Books.

Szasz, T. S. (1977). *The theology of medicine. The political-philosophical foundations of medical ethics.* New York: Harper & Row.

Taieb, O., Flament, M. F., Corcos, M., Jeammet, P., Basquin, M., Mazet, P., & Cohen, D. (2001). Electroconvulsive therapy in adolescents with mood disorder. Patients' and parents' attitudes. *Psychiatry Research, 104,* 183–190.

Taieb, O., Flament, M. F., Chevret, S., Jeammet, P., Allilaire, J. F., Mazet, P., & Cohen, D. (2002). Clinical relevance of electroconvulsive therapy (ECT) in adolescents with severe mood disorder. Evidence from a follow-up study. *European Psychiatry, 17,* 206–212.

Tanney, B. L. (1986). Electroconvulsive therapy and suicide. *Suicide and Life Threatening Behavior, 16,* 116–140.

Taylor, P. J. (1983). Consent, competency and ECT. A psychiatrist's view. *Journal of Medical Ethics, 9,* 146–151.

Taylor, J. R., Tompkins, R., Demers, R., & Anderson, D. (1982). Electroconvulsive therapy and memory dysfunction. Is there evidence for prolonged defects? [review]. *Biological Psychiatry, 17,* 1169–1193.

Taylor, M., Sierles, F. S., & Abrams, R. (1985). *General hospital psychiatry.* New York: Free Press.

Tharyan, P., & Adams, C.E. (2002). Electroconvulsive therapy for schizophrenia. *Cochrane Database System Review 2,* CD00076.

Thase, M. E. (1999). Redefining antidepressant efficacy toward long-term recovery. *The Journal of Clinical Psychiatry, 60* (Suppl. 6), 15–19.

Thase, M. E. (Ed.). (2003a). New approaches to managing difficult-to-treat depressions. *The Journal of Clinical Psychiatry, 64* (Suppl. 1), 1–31.

Thase, M. E. (2003b). Effectiveness of antidepressants. Comparative remission rates. *Journal of Clinical Psychiatry, 64* (Suppl. 2), 3–7.

Thienhaus, O. J., Margletta, S., & Bennett, J. A. (1990). A study of the clinical efficacy of maintenance ECT. *The Journal of Clinical Psychiatry, 51,* 141–144.

Thomas, D. L. L. (1954). Prognosis of treatment with electrical treatment. *British Medical Journal, 2,* 950–954.

Thomas M. (1984). *Home from 7-North, A psychological journey.* Roslyn Heights NY: Libra Publishers.

Thompson, J. W., & Blaine, J. D. (1987). Use of ECT in the United States in 1975 and 1980. *The American Journal of Psychiatry, 144,* 557–562.

Thompson, J. W., Weiner, R. D., & Mayers, C. P. (1994). Use of ECT in the United States in 1975, 1980, 1986. *The American Journal of Psychiatry, 151,* 1657–1661.

Thuppal, M., & Fink, M. (1999). Electroconvulsive therapy and mental retardation. *The Journal of ECT, 15,* 140–149.

UK ECT Review Group (2003). Efficacy and safety of electroconvulsive therapy in depressive disorders. A systematic review and meta-analysis. *Lancet, 361,* 799–808.

Ulett, G. A., Smith, K., & Gleser, G. C. (1956). Evaluation of convulsive and sub-convulsive shock therapies utilizing a control group. *The American Journal of Psychiatry, 112,* 795–802.

United Nations General Assembly. (1948). *Your human rights: The universal declaration of human rights proclaimed by the United Nations, December 10, 1948.* New York: Ellmer Publishers, 1950.

United Nations General Assembly. (1991). *Principles for the protection of persons with mental illness and for the improvment of mental health care, December 17, 1991,* A/RES/46/119, http://www.un.org/documents/ga/res/46/a46r119.htm

Vaeth, J. M. (Ed.). (1979). *Combined effects of chemotherapy and radiotherapy on normal tissue tolerance.* Basel: Karger.

Valenstein, E. S. (1980). *The psychosurgery debate: Scientific, legal, and ethical perspectives.* San Francisco: W.H. Freeman & Co.

Valenstein, E. S. (1986). *Great and desperate cures: The rise and decline of psychosurgery and other radical treatments for mental illness.* New York: Basic Books.

Van Atta, W. (1961). *Shock treatment.* Garden City, NY: Doubleday & Co.

van der Wurff, Stek, H.L., Hoogendåjk, W.J.G., Beerman A.T.F. (2004). Discrepancy between opinion and attitude on use of ECT by old age psychiatrists. *The Journal of ECT, 20,* 37–41

van Houtte, P., Klastersky, J., & Rocmans, P. (Eds.). (1999). *Progress and perspective in the treatment of lung cancer.* Berlin: Springer Verlag.

van Waarde, J. A., Stolker, J. J., Vander Mask, R. C. (2001). ECT in mental retardation: A review. *The Journal of ECT., 17,* 236–243.

Volavka, J., Feldstein, S., Abrams, R., & Fink, M. (1972). EEG and clinical change after bilateral and unilateral electroconvulsive therapy. *Electroencephalogr Clin Neurophysiology, 32,* 631–639.

Vonnegut M. (1975). *The Eden express.* New York: Praeger.

Walter, G., & Rey, J. M. (1997). Epidemiological study of the use of ECT in adolescents. *Journal of the American Academy of Child and Adolescent Psychiatry, 36,* 809–815.

Walter, G., Rey, J. M., & Starling, J. (1997). Experience, knowledge and attitudes of child psychiatrists about ECT in the young. *Austalian and New Zealand Journal of Psychiatry, 31,* 676–681.

Walter, G., Koster, K., & Rey, J. M. (1999). ECT in adolescents, experience, knowledge and attitudes of recipients. *Journal of the American Academy of Child and Adolescent Psychiatry, 38,* 594–599.

Weeks, D., Freeman, C. P. L., & Kendell, R. E. (1980). ECT. III. Enduring cognitive deficits? *The British Journal of Psychiatry, 137,* 26–37.

Wennström, M., Hellsten, J. & Tingström, A. (2004). Electroconvulsive seizures induce proliferation of NG2-expressing glia cells in adult rat amygdala. *Biological Psychiatry, 55,* 464–471.

West, E. D. (1981). Electric convulsion therapy in depression: A double-blind controlled trial. *British Medical Journal, 282,* 355–357.

Wheeler Vega, J. A., Mortimer, A. M., & Tyson, P. J. (2000). Somatic treatment of psychotic depression. Review and recommendations for practice. *Journal of Clinical Psychopharmacology, 20,* 504–519.

Wood, D. A., & Burgess, P. M. (2003). Epidemiological analysis of electroconvulsive therapy in Victoria, Australia. *Australian and New Zealand Journal of Psychiatry, 37,* 307–311.

World Health Organization. (1996). *Mental health law. Ten basic principles.* Geneva.

World Medical Association. (2000). *Declaration of Helsinki.* France: Ferney-Voltaire Cedex.

World Medical Association. (2003). Declaration of Helsinki, ethical principles for medical research involving human subjects. Latest revision Edinburgh Scotland, note of clarification Washington, D.C. 2002. www.wma.net.

World Psychiatric Association. (1978). Declaration of Hawaii. *Journal of Medical Ethics 4,* 71–73.

World Psychiatric Association. (2003). www.wpanet.org.

Wyden, P. (1998). *Conquering schizophrenia: A father, his son and the medical breakthrough.* New York: Alfred A Knopf.

Yardley, J. (2002). Friends and family ask jury to spare Texas mother's life. Letters. *New York Times,* March 14.

Zinkler, M., & Priebe, S. (2002). Detention of the mentally ill in Europe—A review. *Acta Psychiatrica Scandinavica, 106,* 3–8.

Ziskind, E., Sommerfeld-Ziskind, E., & Ziskind, L. (1945). Metrazol and electroconvulsive therapy of the affective psychoses. *Archives of Neurology and Psychiatry, 53,* 212–217.

Author Biographies

Jan-Otto Ottosson M.D., Ph.D.

Jan-Otto Ottosson is professor emeritus of psychiatry. He received his M.D. in 1951 and Ph.D.
in 1960 at the Karolinska Institute in Stockholm.
He has been professor of psychiatry and chairman at the university departments of psychiatry
in Umeå and Göteborg between 1963–1991. He
served as editor-in-chief of the *Acta Psychiatrica
Scandinavica* from 1983 to 1997 and was a
member of the editorial board of the quarterly
scientific journal *Convulsive Therapy*.

In 1989, he attended an intensive bioethics
course at Georgetown University that became
the basis for his thinking on the ethics of ECT. In different roles, he has been
a leader in the application of ethical principles to health care—chairman of
the Delegation of Medical Ethics of the Swedish Society of Medicine, chairman of the Ethics Research Committee of the University of Göteborg,
Swedish delegate to the European Association of Centers for Medical Ethics,
and an expert of the Biomedical Ethics Council of the Swedish government.
As Swedish delegate to the World Psychiatric Association he contributed to
the approval of the Hawaii Declaration, the first code of ethics in psychiatry. He was general secretary of the Swedish Parliamentary Priorities
Commission.

His textbook of clinical psychiatry is widely used in Swedish medical
schools and has appeared in several editions since first published in 1983.
His book on the Swedish history of psychiatry was published in 2003, and
he has edited the *Scientific Basis of Art of Medicine* describing the patient-
doctor relationship, published by the Swedish Council on Technology
Assessment in Health Care in 1999. He is an honorary member of the
Swedish Psychiatric Association and the Swedish Society of Medicine and
received the Erik Strömgren medal of the Psychiatric Institute in Aarhus,
Denmark in 1987.

Max Fink, M.D.

Dr. Fink received his M.D. from New York University College of Medicine in 1945. He served as a medical officer in the US Army, 1946–47 and was certified as a specialist in neurology (1952), psychoanalysis (1953), and psychiatry (1954). He was appointed Research Professor of Psychiatry at Washington University in 1962, and then at New York Medical College (1966 to 1972), and since 1972 at SUNY at Stony Brook, where he is Professor of Psychiatry and Neurology Emeritus. Since 1997, he has also been on the faculty of the Albert Einstein College of Medicine and the LIJ-Hillside Medical Center.

His studies of ECT began at Hillside Hospital in 1952, and he has published broadly on predictors of outcome, effects on EEG and speech, hypotheses of the mode of action, and how to achieve effective treatment. In 1972, with Drs. Seymour Kety and James McGaugh, he organized a conference on the biology of convulsive therapy, under NIMH auspices which resulted in the volume *Psychobiology of Convulsive Therapy* (1974). In 1979, he published the textbook *Convulsive Therapy: Theory and Practice* (Raven Press, 306 pp.).

He established *CONVULSIVE THERAPY*, a quarterly scientific journal, in 1985 (now renamed the *Journal of ECT*). From 1975 to 1978, and again from 1987 to 1990, he was a member of the Task Forces on Electroconvulsive Therapy of the American Psychiatric Association. In 1995–1996, he chaired the Task Force on Ambulatory ECT of the Association for Convulsive Therapy. In 1999, he published the trade book *ELECTROSHOCK: Restoring the Mind* (Oxford University Press, NY) that was re-issued in paperback in 2002.

He has received many prize awards for his research into the mode of action and improvements in ECT, including the Electroshock Research Association Award (1956), the A.E. Bennett award of the Society of Biological Psychiatry (1958), the Anna Monika Prize award for research into depressive illness (1979), the Laszlo Meduna Prize of the Hungarian National Institute for Nervous and Mental Disease (1986), the Gold Medal award of the Society of Biological Psychiatry (1988), and Lifetime Achievement Awards of the *Psychiatric Times* (1995) and of the Society of Biological Psychiatry (1996).

In psychopharmacology, he established a classification of psychoactive drugs by digital computer analysis of EEG and has contributed to the study of narcotic antagonists and of cannabis.

In 1997 he organized the 4-hospital collaborative study group known as CORE under grants from NIMH. *Catatonia: A Clinician's Guide to Diagnosis and Treatment*, a joint effort with Prof Michael A. Taylor of University of Michigan, was published by Cambridge University Press in 2003. He and Dr. Taylor are now collaborating on *Melancholia*, a text to be published by Cambridge University Press.

Index